WHY SHOULD I GO TO BUDAPEST

WHY SHOULD I GO TO ↳
BUDAPEST

THE CITY YOU DEFINITELY NEED TO
VISIT BEFORE YOU TURN 30 (OR 130)

(m)

THIS IS WHY!

Budapest is a city of contrasts: the hills of Buda versus the flat streets of Pest, the green contrasted by the concrete, the rich history as opposed to the modern capital, East versus West. This is what makes a visit to Budapest so special: the city has the familiarity of being a major European city (albeit at an accessible scale) but is, in a way, like an innocent young child facing the new world.

Budapest functions as an island within the country, in terms of both its amenities and residents. The city bursts with creativity that is reflected in every corner – in the cafés and restaurants, the shops, the architecture, and the public spaces. It is a welcoming, international community, where you can freely stop people in the streets to ask for directions, even though it's nearly impossible to get lost with the elaborate public transport system.

Climb Gellért Hill for the best views and a bit of exercise, sit by the Danube River with a refreshing drink, and wander the old cobblestones of Buda Castle like the kings of old. Take in the history that is all around, let yourself go in the vibrant nightlife, or enjoy a cosy night in one of the many unique cafés and bars. Go shopping for vintage treasures or high fashion, or take a walk in the woods of the Buda Hills. Lose yourself in art halls and museums, or take glamorous pictures in magical spots, unwind in a thermal bath, or watch an old classic in one of the independent cinemas. In other words: discover *your* Budapest.

CONTENTS

DISTRICTS 8
PRACTICAL INFO 12

WHEN TO TRAVEL 28
LIFE IN BUDAPEST 38

FOOD AND DRINKS 104
GOING OUT 126

GREEN BUDAPEST 172
OUTSIDE OF BUDAPEST 184

SHOPPING 140

Index 188
Who made this book? 191-192

DISTRICTS

Budapest has a total of 23 districts, each with its own local government. However, only half of them are located within the main circular road, and the others are mainly residential. To make it easier to navigate the city, some districts have been grouped together in this book.

Buda Castle District

The Castle District is the historic part of the city. As it is located on a hill and it is paved with cobblestones, it is best explored on foot. In this part of Budapest, you'll find the Royal Palace that housed the kings of Hungary, as well as the iconic Fisherman's Bastion and the Matthias Church. Descend via the tranquil Castle Garden Bazaar.

Újbuda

Even though the 11th district Újbuda ('New Buda') is one of the largest of Budapest, you will likely only see a small section of it during your stay. Its most important landmark is Gellért Hill, with the Citadel and the *Statue of Liberty*. At its foot, you will find the famous Gellért Spa and the start of the Bartók Béla Boulevard with its many galleries, bars, and restaurants, where you can enjoy an evening surrounded by locals.

Belváros, Lipótváros & Erzsébetváros

The city centre (Belváros) and Lipótváros are an overlap of districts 5 and 6 which, together with the 7th district (Erzsébetváros), form the bustling heart of Budapest. This is where you will find sights like the Parliament Building, Liberty Square, St. Stephen's Basilica and the Great Synagogue – and, therefore, most of your fellow visitors. Make sure to look up, as you wander the city, to marvel at Budapest's exceptional architectural details.

Andrássy út & Városliget

The design of the main boulevard, Andrássy út, was based on Paris' Champs Élysées. It separates districts 6 and 7, and its inner part is flanked by high-end shops, with villas and embassies towards the City Park (Városliget) and Heroes' Square (Hősök tere). The City Park houses not only the Vajdahunyad Castle but also the House of Hungarian Music, the Museum of Ethnography, the Zoo, and the National Circus.

Józsefváros & Ferencváros

Districts 8 and 9 used to be rougher areas, but nowadays they are the hub of up-and-coming Budapest. Józsefváros and Ferencváros are filled with little gems in terms of shops, bars, and things to do. The Botanical Gardens, as well as the Holocaust Museum can be found here too.

Óbuda & Margaret Island

Technically, Margaret Island is not part of any district, but it is nice to combine with a trip to Óbuda ('Old Buda'). Margaret Island has a circumference of 5 km (with an excellent running track) and is mainly a large park where people come to have a picnic, do yoga or read a book. You will also find a sanctuary for birds of prey, a petting zoo and Japanese Gardens on the island. Crossing over to Buda, Óbuda holds the largest remnant of Roman times: Aquincum.

Buda Hills

Away from the busy city centre, the quiet green of the Buda Hills is a great way to escape for a bit, with Normafa as a good starting point. You can walk up to the Elisabeth Lookout and enjoy the view, take a ride on the Children's Railway or just go for a hike.

PRACTICAL INFO

TRAVEL

With its roughly 1.7 million residents, Budapest is one of the largest cities in the region. The inhabitants are spread out over a territory of 525 m2, where they can get around quite comfortably thanks to the city's vast network of public transport: four metro lines, trams, buses, trains, trolley buses, and a bicycle sharing scheme all ensure that you can always get to where you need to be.
The BKK (Budapest Transport Centre) has a user-friendly website and app containing a useful travel planner to check timetables and plan your journey. You can buy your tickets or passes through the app, but in that case, you will need to scan the QR-code of any vehicle you enter to validate your ticket.
If you plan on using public transport on a regular basis, it's best to buy one of the multi-day pass options. If you use single tickets, you need to validate one ticket per transfer – with underground transfers, from metro line to metro line, as the only exception.
Getting to the city centre from the airport is relatively easy. You can either choose the special airport shuttle bus that takes you directly to Deák Ferenc tér for an extra fee, or you could take bus 200E to Kőbánya-Kispest metro station, where you transfer onto metro line M3 to take you into the heart of Budapest. Both journeys will take around forty minutes. Each of the four main train and bus stations is served by metro lines.

You don't have to worry about getting around late at night, as tram 6 – which covers the heart of the city – runs all night, and there is a dense network of night buses in place.

Cycling in the city is getting more and more common, as cycle lanes are increasing in numbers, so don't hesitate to have a go at cycling the city. Riding a bike allows you to explore Budapest from a different angle, and there are many good bike rental shops around town, such as Dynamo Bike & Bake or BudaBike. The city bikes MOL BuBi can easily be spotted by their bright green colour. After registration, you can purchase a pass for a symbolic amount, after which each half hour in between dockings is free. Better check out the nearest docking station to your destination in advance!

To fully take in the view along the riverbanks, you can jump aboard one of the sightseeing cruises offered by the Hungarian Boating Association (MAHART). With a hop-on-hop-off day ticket you can zigzag your way across both banks at your leisure. If you have more time, you can take a boat all the way to the scenic towns of Szentendre or Visegrád up the river.

Budapest has some spectacular modes of transport. One you shouldn't miss is the funicular that takes you up to Buda Castle. This UNESCO World Heritage site had its first ride in 1870 and can now be explored in its full, restored glory. Should you venture into the Buda Hills, you can take tram line 60, which is a special cog railway and a sight in its own right. Once you're on top, make sure to see the Children's Railway for yourself: this train line is fully operated by Scouts and allows you a ride through the woods with astonishing views. Descend from János Hill back to the city by chairlift (*libegő*) – if you are not afraid of heights, that is!

WHERE TO STAY

Czakó Bed&Breakfast

1016, Czakó u. 15, Buda Castle District, czakokert.com

The Buda side of the city often gets overlooked for accommodation, but a stay in Czakó, close to Buda Castle, is well worth considering. Charming and cosy, you'll also find a restaurant and garden at Czakó, and on weekends there's a farmer's market. If you want a taste of the countryside within the city, this is a good option.

Shantee House

1113, Takács Menyhért u. 33, Újbuda, backpackersbudapest.hu

Shantee House emphasises nature and exudes creativity. It is close to the Kelenföld Train Station, so it's a good option for those arriving by train. It's ideal if you'd like to stay somewhere quieter with access to public transport to the city centre. You can book anything from dorm room to private yurt, and both bikes and skateboards are available for rent.

Wombat's City Hostel

1061, Király u. 20, Belváros, wombats-hostels.com/Budapest

Wombat's Budapest's location is right in the middle of the hustle and bustle of the Jewish quarter. Only a short walk from many good restaurants, bars, and nightlife, this hostel is a great option for backpackers or urban explorers who like to meet new people and hit the town with them. They also offer female-only dormitories.

Netizen Budapest Centre

1074, Rákóczi út 54, Belváros, netizenbudapestcentre.hu

You'll find this hostel on the edge of the ever-busy Jewish quarter. It is very easy to reach by public transport, as it can be found right next to the important tram and metro station on Blaha Lujza tér. The interior has a vibrant, modern design, and inside you'll find a cafe and bar as well. They also offer female-only dormitories

Charm Hotel Budapest

1056, Só u. 6, Belváros, charmhotelbudapest.com

Is comfort more your style than a hostel in the middle of the party district? Formerly known as the Boutique Hotel, Charm Hotel can be found just around the corner from a major shopping street, the Central Market Hall, the Danube, and the iconic Liberty Bridge. If you prefer restful accommodations while being close to the heart of the city, you can find one right there.

Paulay Downtown Apartments

1061, Paulay Ede u. 13, Belváros, paulay-downtown-apartments. inbudapesthotels.com

Paulay Downtown Apartments are technically in the Jewish Quarter, but they are more family focused and located in a street that is noticeable quieter than most of the district. Standard rooms come with a kitchenette, and family-sized rooms are available as well.

Vagabond SOHO

1073, Kertész u. 25, Belváros, vagabondhotels.com/ location/soho

You might think it would seem impossible to combine close proximity to nightlife with coming home to your own little apartment without loud roommates or shared bathrooms, but Vagabond SOHO fits this description perfectly. It's located just inside the Jewish Quarter.

Onefam Budapest

1075, Rumbach Sebestyén u. 6, Belváros, onefamhostels.com/budapest-onefam-hostel-budapest

This hostel in the heart of the party district aims to organise as many activities as possible to make sure that their visitors will leave them having made new friends and having had a proper taste of the Budapest bars and clubs. An open mindset is a must if you want to stay here.

The Hive Party Hostel

1074, Dob u. 19, Belváros, thehive.hu

This hostel embraces its identity wholeheartedly: why leave your hostel to go partying with your new friends and roommates if you can get the party started in the hostel itself? Located in the Jewish Quarter, there are plenty of places to stop by late at night when coming back from the bars or clubs.
Corvin Point offers hotel rooms and small

Corvin Point

1082, Nap u. 4, Józsefváros, corvinpoint.com

apartments close to tram and metro, and pretty much next to a shopping centre. Its location is within easy walking distance of the busy part of the city centre. Parking spaces are provided, making it a good pick if you're travelling by car.

Flow Spaces

1093, Gönczy Pál u. 2, Belváros, flowspaces.hu

Close to the busy city centre, but not quite in it, Flow Spaces offers both private rooms and dormitories (female-only available as well) close to the Danube River and Central Market Hall. There are a few university buildings nearby, so in the area around Flow Spaces you'll find a lot of students, and fun, affordable places to hang out in.

Maverick Urban Lodge

1093, Lónyai u. 31, Ferencváros, mavericklodges.com/en/urban-lodge-budapest-hostel

Maverick Urban Lodge offers both private rooms and beds in dormitories (female-only available) close to the Danube River, within walking distance of a lot of nice restaurants and bars. But before you head out, make sure to check the bar on the ground floor. The surrounding area is often vibrant, and a short tram or bus ride will take you anywhere in the city centre.

GOOD TO KNOW

Money

Hungary has not yet entered the Eurozone, and the local currency is called the Forint (HUF). Most credit and debit cards, as well as contactless payments, are widely accepted in shops, bars, cafés, and restaurants in Budapest. However, if you go to any type of market, or venture outside of town, you might still need to pay in cash, which is why it's worth carrying some. Additionally, you might get a better exchange rate for cash than your bank or the payment terminal will offer. If you need to withdraw cash, avoid kerbside ATMs as costs are excessive, it's best to use the ones inside banks. Beware of exchange offices in tourist areas or at the airport, as rates might still not be in your favour.

Tipping

A 10% tip is common in bars and restaurants or for other services – although it's always best to check the bill, as a service charge is often included.

Opening hours

Hungarians change the opening hours of their establishments at the drop of a hat, which is why it is always best to double-check opening times before heading somewhere. Museums are usually closed on Mondays (but free on public holidays), and small shops tend to be closed on Saturday afternoons and Sundays.
Shops, except for some smaller 24-hour shops, are generally closed on national

holidays. Cafés and restaurants may choose to stay open, but it is best to check their website in advance. If a national holiday falls on a Tuesday or a Thursday, the bridging day is also part of the holiday. Typically, Sunday opening times apply on these days.

Cuisine

Budapest is a true metropolis where you can find all kinds of foods. Moreover, it's one of the best cities to eat in if you have any kind of allergy or intolerance, and it is a definite haven for sugar-free options.

That however is not true for Hungarian cuisine generally, which is characterised by heavy dishes loaded with greasy meat and potatoes. It is the home of goulash, peppers, and dried salami with a shot of *pálinka* (a strong fruit brandy) on the side. Hungary is the country of a two-course hot lunch with a soup for a starter — which is why you will find many restaurants offer fixed-priced daily lunch menus.

In Hungary, soup can be cold and fruity, and pasta may be sweet. Any delicacy with poppy seeds is a must, as well as the many cakes in coffee houses — a legacy of the Habsburg era. Highlights to look out for are *flódni* (a layered cake with poppy seeds, walnut, apple, and prune jam), *eszterházi* (walnut cake) and *somlói* (a sponge cake with walnuts and chocolate sauce). Don't miss the classic chimney cake (*kürtős kalács* — preferably one from a random metro station booth, rather than a fancy one with ice cream) and the *lángos* (a flat, deep-fried flat bread with sour cream and cheese). If you're in a supermarket, try and find *túrórudi* (a cold, chocolate-covered cottage cheese classic).

Hungary also has excellent wines, and their most famous are from the Tokaj-Hegyalja historical wine region in the east of the country. However, if you get the chance, make sure to try wines from the wide range of other regions,

such as Villány, Badacsony or Eger, the latter having the renowned *bikavér* (bull's blood). Closest to Budapest are the rich vineyards of Etyek and Budafok, both accessible by public transport. If you are in town in September, make sure to check on the dates of various wine festivals (the one at Buda Castle is usually early in the month).

Don't be surprised if you see locals mixing their wine with sparkling water; the mixer *fröccs* is very popular. Depending on the ratio of the ingredients, *fröccs* takes on different names. The *hosszúlépés* (long step) consists of one part wine and two parts water and is most common. The *viceházmester* (vice concierge) has two parts wine and three parts water.

As for going out: 're-cup' systems have become the norm in most party venues in Budapest. That means that you pay a deposit for the cup your drink comes in with your first round, and you'll bring it back to reuse it for the next drink. Don't forget to bring it back in when you are heading home, to get your deposit back. Some venues will give you a token instead of money, to use the next time you are in one of the associated bars.

Language

Hungarian is a notoriously difficult language to learn. It shares roots with Finnish and Estonian, and is a linguistic island, surrounded by Slavic and Germanic languages in neighbouring countries. In most situations – especially in tourist areas – you will get by with English, as most Budapesters speak it to some degree, especially the younger generations. Traditionally, members of the baby boom generation and older are often more comfortable speaking German, as that used to be the more common foreign language taught in school because of the geographical proximity of Austria and cultural ties. If you want to sound like a local, use *szia* (pronounced see-ya), which means 'hi' and can be used both to greet someone and to say goodbye, which is why you might hear Hungarians use 'hello' as a farewell instead of 'bye'. Finally, a disclaimer for when you overhear people on the phone seemingly being very improper: *puszi* translates to 'kisses' and is also used informally as a way to say goodbye.

BUDAPEST IN SPRING

'Spring wind floods water,' claims a Hungarian folk song. It can be a fickle season, with cold, rainy days or a hot, sunny pre-summer. Even snow during Easter is not unheard of. Still, spring in Budapest has its own perks: the parks are sprouting green and there are flowers all around, the city awakes from its winter slumber and a general cheer descends upon Budapest. It starts with the carnival season, which is traditionally celebrated in Mohács, in the South of the country with *busójárás*. The main focus during the four-day festival is on big, masked monsters, *busó*, who walk around in order to scare away evil spirits and thus winter itself, or so they say.

Easter also has traditional elements, the most important one being the 'sprinkling of the ladies': for women not to wither the next year, men go around sprinkling water or perfume on them. In return, they receive a red Easter egg, a shot of *pálinka*, or money. Good Friday and Easter Monday are public holidays, as well as 15th March, when the revolution and war of independence of 1848-49 against the Habsburgs is commemorated and protests and political rallies are held all over the city.

BUDAPEST IN SUMMER

Summer in the city has a lifestyle of its own. As days are hot and nights often don't cool down at the height of the season, you can be outside roaming the streets late at night, sitting along the Danube or enjoying a drink in one of the garden pubs without as much as a shiver. Daytime can be scorching, which is why a nice hat and sunscreen are strongly recommended. Fortunately, there are many places around town where you can refill your water bottle for free, and if it gets unbearable, you can take a dip in a pool at one of the many bathhouses. Don't be deceived, though, as summer is often accompanied by storms, which can cause the air to cool down a few degrees. So it is best to pack a variety of clothes. Don't miss the national holiday celebrations on 20th August, with one of Europe's biggest fireworks displays over the Danube.

Summer is also the season of music festivals, with many throughout the country. In Budapest you have the famous Sziget Festival of course, typically held in the second week of August. If that is your cup of tea, it is definitely worth planning your visit around it — otherwise it might be wise to choose a different time for your trip to the city, as Budapest can be quite busy during the festival.

BUDAPEST IN AUTUMN

Autumn is probably the best time to visit Budapest, especially in September and early October. The balmy weather usually lasts for quite a while, and has all the advantages of actual summer, with the extra charm of being able to enjoy the warm atmosphere of the various indoor bars and restaurants in the evening. With schools opening again, the city gets back to its regular rhythm and opening hours and awakes from its summer slumber. With the leaves changing colour, it is the perfect time for a walk in the Buda Hills to admire the breathtaking landscape with all its shades of yellow. The first of November, All Saints' Day, is a national holiday in Hungary. Take the opportunity to join the locals at the cemetery at night, when they light candles for their departed, filling the otherwise sombre location with a warm glow. The historic Fiumei út cemetery is especially beautiful.

23rd October is another public holiday, commemorating the 1956 revolution against Soviet troops. Shops are usually closed, and many political rallies are traditionally held throughout the city.

Autumn is also the season of harvest, when the slopes of vineyards all over Hungary are heavy with ripe fruit, and the first wine of the year is bottled for you to taste at various wine festivals all over the city, most famous (and largest) is held at Buda Castle in September.

BUDAPEST IN WINTER

Winter wonderland in Budapest is like no other: December, in particular, is a magical month. Hungarians take Advent very seriously, with not only decorations and lights all around, but also many Christmas markets, the biggest of which has been voted the best in Europe for several years. Mingle with the jolly crowd, treat yourself to a glass of mulled wine, and marvel at the various stalls with traditional craftsmanship on display. You won't regret staying for New Year's Eve, as Hungarians have a way of entering the new year with a bang: silly outfits and wigs, party horns in various sizes and colours, and the whole city turning into one big dance floor. Christmas, Boxing Day, and New Year's Day are national holidays to be taken into consideration when booking a trip.

The jaw-dropping light show at St Stephen's Basilica is an absolute must.

Get your skates on directly in front of Vajdahunyad Castle between late November and mid-February. City Park Ice Rink is one of the oldest and largest in Europe. It's filled with water during the summer months, when it serves as a boating lake. When it's frozen over in winter, you can marvel at the sights around you whilst skating.

Taking a dip in one of the many famous baths during winter is an experience not to be missed. Jumping from one of the indoor pools into the outside pool will wake you up properly. It is also the perfect time to enjoy the inviting saunas and steam baths.

HISTORY

Although the city of Budapest has only recently celebrated its 150th birthday, its history dates back to the Romans, who originally founded it, and Buda Castle could tell fascinating stories of Hungary's former kings. Since Hungarians are fiercely proud of their heritage, it is good to consider your visit to Budapest from a historical perspective, as it may help you gain a better understanding of what you see.

Aquincum

The history of the city starts in Óbuda ('Old Buda'), now the 3rd district. In the 1st century CE, the Romans settled at this location, building the *castrum* (fortified camp) called Aquincum with a legion of 6,000 men. However, archaeologists discovered that the area had been inhabited by the Celtic Evarisks long before the Romans set foot there. Artefacts discovered at the site are on display in the Budapest History Museum. The Celtic Evarisks had to make way for the Romans, who chose this strategic location because of the Danube that formed a natural border for the region known at the time as Pannonia (and the outer border of the Empire). Exploring Óbuda, you will find many remnants of this era, including the amphitheatre in Nagyszobat utca, and the excavation site, which still bears the name of the ancient settlement.

Magyars

Although we cannot be quite sure when the Magyars first entered the Carpathian Basin, it is generally agreed that the process started around the year 895 CE and that by the early 900s, they had the whole area under their control. At the time the Magyars arrived on the scene, the area was home to various tribes and peoples. Most famous were the Huns, with their notorious king Attila who had his seat built in what is now Budapest. The exact origins of the Magyars are open to much debate, but since the Hungarian language shares roots with Finnish and Estonian, it is widely believed that the origins of this nomadic group lie in the Ural Mountains. And although in the end the Magyars ultimately defeated the Huns and took control of the land, both live on in the country's folk tales. According to one popular legend, Hungary was founded by two brothers, Hunor and Magor, who, while chasing a magical deer, stumbled upon two fair maidens they then married, founding the Hun and Magyar tribes. And while Hungarians refer to themselves as *Magyars* (and the country's name is *Magyarország* in Hungarian), on an international level, the association with the Huns endures.

Turkish baths

One thing you must try when you're in the city is a visit to one of the grand thermal baths of Budapest. Bathing culture has deep roots in Hungarian society that go back to the 150 years of Ottoman occupation in the 16th and 17th centuries. Not much is left of this mark on the city's history, but some bathhouses remain in all their glory. As Hungary is rich in beneficial thermal springs, you can experience them throughout the city. Rudas, originally built in 1556 at the foot of the Gellért Hill, is one of the best preserved.

Revolution

After the Ottomans were finally driven out of what was left of Buda and Pest with the aid of the Habsburgs in 1686, the liberators overstayed their welcome – a pattern that recurred throughout the rest of Hungarian history. Hungary became part of the Habsburg Empire. Hungarians finally joined the revolution as part of a wave of uprisings across Europe in 1848. The outbreak in Budapest on 15th March is now a national holiday, and the events of that day are well known to all, as is their key figure, poet Sándor Petőfi. Even though the revolution and war of independence failed, they played a significant role in the Austro-Hungarian Compromise of 1867 (*Kiegyezés*) that established the dual monarchy of Austria-Hungary.

Buda and Pest

It took Buda and Pest a good number of centuries to rebuild after the Ottoman occupation, but they were back on their feet and thriving at the start of the 19th century. During the Great Flood of 1838, a significant portion of Pest was destroyed. In the years that followed, the cityscape we now know came into existence. While Pest became the commercial hub of the country, Buda was the political capital. Especially after the Austro-Hungarian Monarchy was established, both parts of the city grew exponentially. So much so that it made sense to unite them into one city. Which is why on 17th November 1873, Pest, Buda, and Óbuda were united to create the new capital, Budapest.

The Millennium

When exploring the sights of Budapest, you will often come across the number 896. This number refers to the settlement of the Magyars in the Carpathian Basin, but ultimately, it refers to the Millennium celebrations in 1896. Hungarians know how to throw a party, and to celebrate a thousand years of Hungarian presence in the Carpathian Basin, Budapest underwent a construction boom to be completed in time for the important year. This is when monuments like Heroes' Square, Liberty Bridge, the first underground (now metro line M1), and Vajdahunyad Castle were constructed. The majority of celebrations took place in the City Park, where visitors could marvel at a thousand years of Hungarian history on display.

Trianon

If you look at maps of Hungary from before WWI, you will see a very different image of Europe. Hungary was among the five largest countries at the time, even without adding the Austro-part of the monarchy. All that changed after the Treaty of Versailles, which concluded the war that Hungary was on the losing side of. In a separate treaty, signed at the Palace of Trianon in Versailles, Hungary was divided and lost 71 per cent of its former territory to neighbouring countries, resulting in many Hungarians being detached from their country. Many large industrial cities were suddenly lost, which explains the disproportionate size and influence of Budapest (and its Parliament Building) in comparison with the rest of the country.

Ghetto

Before WWII, a large Jewish community resided in the heart of Budapest. Nothing illustrates this better than the presence of the Grand Synagogue in Wesselényi utca: it is the second-largest in the world and able to host three thousand worshippers. From 1938 onwards, a series of anti-Jewish laws were passed, limiting the freedom of the community. Although Hungary sided with Germany in WWII, Budapest protected its Jewish citizens initially. That ended with the German invasion in 1944, after which the inner part of the 5th district was made into a ghetto on 29th November. Deportations from Budapest to Auschwitz started soon after. The antisemitic Hungarian Arrow Cross Party that came into power during the German occupation, was remorseless in its own way, taking men, women, and children from their homes at night, and shooting them into the waters of the Danube. The Shoe Monument near the Parliament Building is a brutal reminder of these victims.

Soviet Liberation

On 13th February 1945, Soviet troops freed a devastated Budapest from Nazi occupation. However, they decided to stay for another 45 years, which meant that Hungary was part of the Eastern Bloc throughout the second half of the 20th century. Hungary never became part of the Soviet Union but remained under its influence until 12th March 1990, when Soviet troops started leaving the country. Rebuilding after WWII was far from easy: apart from the debris and lives lost, Hungary faced hyperinflation of record proportions in 1946. Life in the city was tough, and Stalinism weighed heavily on citizens' everyday lives.

Revolution, again

After Stalin's death, a window of opportunity seemed to open for Hungary to break free from its communist chains. On 23rd October 1956, 100,000 protesters took to Heroes' Square to tear down the dictator's eight-metre-tall statue (with its boots and other Soviet monuments now exhibited in Memento Park). At the same time, another large group of protesters gathered at Kossuth Lajos tér in front of the Parliament Building. The peaceful protest ended the same day, with shots fired into the masses, and people taking up arms. The promising revolution took a turn for the worse when Soviet tanks came to the Communist Party's aid on 5th November, and a few days later the last remnants of resistance were cleared away. 23rd October has been a national holiday since 1989.

European Capital

Because of Soviet influence, Hungary, like most countries from the Eastern Bloc, started its democratic governance with a big handicap. With the EU accession on 1st May 2004 came the promise of a brighter future, with access to more resources. However, Budapest remains a place of polarisation. On the one hand, there is tension between the multicultural, globalised capital and the rest of the country. On the other, Budapest remains a very liberal island in an increasingly conservative society, driven by politics. For this reason, funding for Budapest has become increasingly difficult, which is reflected in the cityscape, where renovation projects are forced to a standstill and new ones are waiting to be started. Still, Budapest keeps its head held high.

SIGHTSEEING

Buda Castle & Fisherman's Bastion

Buda Castle District

Atop its hill, Buda Castle, with its characteristic, green-domed roof, is a marvel to behold from across the river. And it's well worth paying a visit to see it up close too, as its surroundings are brimming with architecture worthy of the kings and queens that once resided here. The palace houses the National Gallery, the Budapest History Museum, and the National Library. Many festivals are held within the castle walls, including the Buda Wine Festival and the Festival of Folk Arts. A stone's throw away, you'll find the Fisherman's Bastion, built for the Millennium celebrations with the sole purpose of being beautiful. From the Bastion, you can catch a nice scenic view of the Pest side. Outside of opening hours, you can walk along the site for free. Next to it is Matthias Church, with its Zsolnay ceramic-tiled roof.

Várkert Bazár

1013, Ybl Miklós tér 2-6, Buda Castle District

Close to Buda Castle, you'll find Várkert Bazár. Várkert translates to 'castle garden' (and Bazár means bazaar). Here you'll find the Castle Gardens, with impressive architecture. It is great for taking a leisurely stroll and enjoying the view, and chances are you'll come across a temporary exhibition, an open-air concert, or a sports event on the big screen. The gardens are especially photogenic during spring and summer.

**Gellért Hill &
Statue of Liberty**

*1118, Citadella stny. 1,
Újbuda*

At the Buda end of the city's iconic Liberty Bridge lies Gellért Hill, named after the influential bishop who met his demise at this spot in 1044. The stairs and walkways leading to the top of the hill provide its visitors with beautiful vistas over the river along the way, as well as a bit of exercise. On top of the hill, you will find the city's citadel and its *Statue of Liberty*: a woman raising a palm leaf as a symbol of liberty and peace.

St. Steven's Basilica

*1051, Szentt István tér 1,
Belváros*

The Basilica, like the square it is located on, is named after the Hungarian king Stephen (*István*), who was the first to convert both himself and his country to Christianity, and whose mummified holy right hand is on display inside. Construction of the Basilica finished in 1896, the Millennium year, which is also why it is exactly 96 metres tall. Entrance to the Basilica is only free on certain days, such as national holidays, but the exterior is impressive enough. In winter, the square is home to one of Europe's largest Christmas markets.

**Liberty Square
(Szabadság tér)**

*1054, Szabadság tér,
Belváros*

This square in the city centre is home to several noteworthy monuments. On one end, you will find a monument symbolising an eagle attacking an angel to commemorate the victims of the German occupation of 1944. It is controversial, as most who died fell victim to the Hungarian

Arrow Cross Party. This is why locals have installed their own 'counter-monument' in front of it, in an attempt to present a more accurate version of the country's history. On the other end of the square, next to the U.S. Embassy, you will find a monument dedicated to the Soviet liberators of 1945. It is accompanied by statues of George H. W. Bush and Ronald Reagan.

Parliament Building

1055, Kossuth Lajos tér 1-3, Belváros

This building right next to the Danube is the second largest Parliament Building in Europe. Construction of this building also ended in 1896, and just like the Basilica it is exactly 96 metres high, symbolising the equality of Church and State. The colours on the outside match those of the Hungarian flag: red, white, and green. The square in front of it was the starting point of the 1956 uprising, and bullet holes in the façades remain visible as silent witnesses.

Vyšehrad

1055, Belváros

When the Hungarian Arrow Cross Party came into power after the German invasion in 1944, they executed thousands of people in less than a year. Many of these executions took place at the banks of the Danube. Here, their victims, most of whom were Jewish, would be ordered, in groups of five, to remove their shoes and all of their clothes. They would be tied together with their shoelaces, and whoever was in the centre was shot, dragging the others into the river. The shoes that remained along the riverbank have been immortalised as a memorial.

Chain Bridge

1051, Belváros

The Chain Bridge was the first permanent bridge over the Danube to connect Buda and Pest in 1849, and it's difficult to imagine the city without it. The name comes from the chains that British engineer William Clark used, allowing the construction to grow and shrink slightly as temperatures change throughout the year. The four lions guarding both ends are said to have no tongue, which — according to urban legend — caused their sculptor to jump into the Danube, having lost the bet saying that his lions were perfect likenesses of the real animal. On the Buda side, at the base of the castle, you will find the Zero Kilometre Stone, from which all distances in the country are measured.

↓ MATTHIAS CHURCH

Heroes' Square & City Park

1146, Hősök tere, Városliget

At the end of the famous Andrassy Boulevard, located between the Museum of Fine Arts and the Hall of Arts, the Heroes' Square was created on the occasion of the Millennium to honour fallen Hungarian heroes. A large pillar on the square supports Archangel Gabriel, with a backdrop of figures representing past Hungarian kings. Behind the square lies the City Park, which was opened at the same time. Here you will, amongst other fairytale-like buildings, find the Vajdahunyad Castle replica, representing architectural styles from various periods. The lake at the base of the castle is suited for boating in summer and showing off your ice-skating skills in winter.

Central Market Hall

1093, Vámház krt. 1-3, Ferencváros

At the Pest end of the city's iconic Liberty Bridge, you will find the Central Market Hall with its colourful Zsolnay ceramic roof. In this wonderful example of 19th-century architecture, you can experience the hustle and bustle that visitors might feel is lacking on the streets. You can get your basic market goods here, such as fresh produce, but it has also become a location known for its wide selection of souvenirs. This is the place to buy all the Hungarian peppers and sausages you would like to bring home.

↓ FISHERMAN'S BASTION   ↓ VAJDAHUNYAD

Margaret Island

Margaret Island

This island in the middle of the Danube serves mainly as a park but is also rich in history and sights. When entering via Margaret Bridge, you are welcomed by a musical fountain with a choreographed show on display every hour from spring to autumn. About halfway onto the island, you will find the ruins of an old convent that housed the namesake of the insula, St. Margaret, the daughter of King Béla III. At the north end, you can relax and take a stroll through the Japanese gardens, rich in plant diversity. Sightseeing can be done by renting a group bike or fetching the old sightseeing train.

MUSEUMS

National Gallery

1014, Szent György tér 2, Buda Castle District, en.mng.hu

Located in the Buda Castle Palace, the architecture of the National Gallery itself is worth a visit. The dome, the highest point of the palace, offers a spectacular view of Budapest. The main museum collection includes historic Hungarian works of art, 18th- and 19th-century paintings, and sculptures from local as well as international masters. The museum also houses a wide range of temporary exhibitions.

Budapest History Museum

1014, Szent György tér 2, Buda Castle District, varmuzeum.hu

Another wing of the Buda Palace houses the Budapest History Museum, which focuses on the past 2,000 years of what is now the Hungarian capital. Roam through a vast labyrinth of rooms with historical artifacts on display, from photos and graphics to furniture, everyday tools, clothing, and books. It offers history lovers a glimpse into the evolution of the city.

Hospital in the Rock

1012, Lovas út 4/c,
Buda Castle District,
sziklakorhaz.eu

Beneath Castle Hill lies a vast network of tunnels, a section of which was used as an emergency hospital during WWII and the revolution of 1956. At the time of the Cold War, it was transformed into a nuclear bunker, but its existence was top secret until 2002. Now it is a museum, you can head down a dark path of history, where the only light came from those putting everything at risk to help others.

National Museum

1088, Múzeum krt. 14-16,
Belváros, mnm.hu

The permanent exhibition of the National Museum focuses on the history of Hungary and significant relics from its past. This is where you will find the Coronation Mantle of the kings, artefacts from the peoples living in the Carpathian Basin from as early as 400,000 BCE, followed by the history of the country up to the modern era, and even a Roman lapidary exhibit. Upon entering, you can visit the Open Repository (free of charge) which contains porcelain, glass, and ceramics.

↓ CAPA CENTRE

↓ MUSEUM OF FINE ARTS

Light Art Museum

1054, Hold u. 13, Belváros, lam.xyz

Enjoy an immersive experience with light as an art form in this innovative approach to the museum concept. You can enjoy the creativity of light artists from around the world, with Instagrammable installations and illusions in the dark. The exhibition changes every two years.

CAPA Centre

1065, Nagymező u. 8, Belváros, capacenter.hu

Hungarian-born photographer Robert Capa became famous for his motto 'If your photographs aren't good enough, you are not close enough,' which he put into practice during the Spanish Civil War, WWII, and the Vietnam War. The museum now bearing his name is home to photo exhibitions by Hungarian artists and photographers from around the world. It is housed in the impressive Ernst House, built in Art Nouveau style.

House of Terror

1062, Andrássy út 60, Andrássy út & Városliget, terrorhaza.hu

Number 60 on Andrássy Avenue has been the scene of the darkest side of humanity in the 20th century. During WWII, it was the seat of the Arrow Cross Party, and later of the Communist Regime's Secret Police. As such, many of the crimes against humanity committed in Hungary over two dictatorial regimes took place at this location. The museum serves as a reminder that freedom is a rare commodity to be treasured, and that these atrocities should never be allowed to happen again.

Museum of Fine Arts

1146, Dózsa György út 41, Andrássy út & Városliget, szepmuveszeti.hu

Flanking Heroes' Square on the north side, the Museum of Fine Arts has the most impressive selection of Egyptian and classical antiquities and artworks from old Hungarian and international masters, including Goya, Titian, and Van Dyck. Alongside the permanent exhibition, several temporary exhibits are on display. If you're lucky, you might even see once-in-a-lifetime collections, such as works by Van Gogh, Manet, or Bosch.

Hall of Arts

1146, Dózsa György út 37, Andrássy út & Városliget, mucsarnok.hu

Opposite the Museum of Fine Arts rises the neoclassical Hall of Arts, as a more modern counterpart to its neighbour on Heroes' Square. The ever-changing repertoire of contemporary Hungarian and international artists, alongside cultural events such as concerts, workshops, and lectures, makes it a popular venue for locals.

↓ CAPA CENTRE

↓ HOUSE OF TERROR

MUSEUMS

House of Music Hungary

1146, Olof Palme stny. 3-5, Andrássy út & Városliget, zenehaza.hu

Even though it only opened its doors in 2021, the House of Music Hungary has become a must-visit for tourists and locals alike. The interactive permanent exhibition, where you can walk through the history of Hungarian and international music with smart headphones that interact with the items on display, is especially popular. Of course, you can try many of the items yourself. The Sound Dome next door grants you an immersive 360-degree visual and sound show.

Museum of Ethnography

1146, Dózsa György út 35, Andrássy út & Városliget, neprajz.hu

The new, modern building that is home to the Museum of Ethnography is the first purpose-built space to show its collection. Designed by NAPUR Architects, it offers a public green space on top of its slanted roof, with the collection below. The museum focuses on Hungarian culture and heritage, giving you a glimpse of rural life in Hungary through the ages, including household items, textiles, and ritual objects.

Ludwig Museum

1095, Komor Marcell u. 1, Ferencváros, ludwigmuseum.hu

If you prefer contemporary art, the rapidly growing collection of the Ludwig Museum, situated in the stylish, modern building of the Palace of Arts, is highly recommended. The museum started with a large donation of progressive works from the 1960s to the 1980s and now has over a thousand pieces on display in its permanent exhibition.

Aquincum

1031, Szentendrei út 135, Óbuda, aquincum.hu

In Roman times, the region that Hungary was founded in was called Pannonia, and the settlement Aquincum played a strategically important role. Over hundreds of years, that settlement grew into the Budapest we know today, but its archaeological remains can still be visited in Óbuda. In icy or very wet weather, only the indoor exhibits are accessible, so it's best to take weather conditions into account when planning your visit to Aquincum.

Memento Park

1222, Balatoni út, szabadkai utca sarok

Even though it is slightly out of the way, Memento Park comes highly recommended if you are interested in 20th-century history. All the relics of the socialist era were banned to this park. They are mostly large statues, including the boots of that of Stalin which was torn down at the start of the revolution on 23rd October 1956, but you'll also find some photographs and other relics in the park.

↓ LIGHT ART MUSEUM

STREET ART

Budapest has a rich palette of street art to discover, and even though it is always fun to stumble upon them by chance, there are a few that you shouldn't miss when visiting the city.

Sissy by Neopaint

Rumbach Sebestyén u. 10, Erzsébetváros

A portrait of the beloved Empress Elisabeth, wife of Franz Josef I, who loved Hungary and was a frequent visitor to their royal palace in Gödöllő. While tensions between Hungary and the Habsburg dynasty were still high, she was – and still is – considered a national treasure, which is why you'll come across lots of references to Sissy in the city, such as her statue on Madách Square nearby.

6:3 by Neopaint

Rumbach Sebestyén u. 10, Erzsébetváros

It was considered the match of the century, England vs Hungary in 1953. Hungary were Olympic champions at the time and had a run of 24 unbeaten games. The match held at Wembley ended in a never-before-seen 3-6 score for Hungary; a defeat that changed English football tactics fundamentally, and a victory that lives on in the hearts of all Hungarians.

Rubik's Cube by Neopaint

Dob u. 10, Erzsébetváros

Although most people have played with it or at least seen one, they may not know it originated in Hungary: the Rubik's Cube, or Magic Cube, named after its inventor, Ernő Rubik. The mural comes with one of the creator's famous quotes, which translates to, 'There is always a solution, sometimes even more than one.'

Budapest isn't so small by Richárd Orosz

Kazinczy u. 45, Erzsébetváros

When you're only in Budapest for a short time, you can easily get overwhelmed by the buzz of the inner city and its night life – even though the capital has so much more to offer. This 20 m2 painting draws attention to just that: Budapest is a lot bigger than just the typical hotspots, and there is a lot to explore, even beyond the city's borders.

Sunrise or Sunset by Neopaint

Kazinczy u. 55, Erzsébetváros

Kazinczy Street has evolved over the years into the beating heart of the district, with big hotspots like Szimpla and Kőleves Kert. This piece of street art gives you a good overview of the wide variety of venues the street has to offer, including cultural sights, restaurants, and bars.

Refugees by Neopaint

Klauzál u. 32, Erzsébetváros

When the war in Ukraine broke out, neighbouring country Hungary took in a large wave of refugees fleeing the conflict. However noble, this didn't come without substantial criticism of Hungary's anti-migration policy that is characterised by fenced-off borders. Hence the UNHCR mural, reminding everyone that help needs to be offered to all refugees, wherever they may come from.

Beautify Budapest by Kata Kerekes

Akácfa u. 27, Erzsébetváros

This 100 m2 mural captures the joy, happy moments, and freedom of true summer in Budapest. The painting was sponsored by Polaroid, which explains the multitude of sunglasses present, but the coolest feature of this piece of art is the paint that was used to make it. With new, intelligent technology, the paint absorbs CO_2 and other harmful substances and therefore has a function of cleaning its environment.

**Angel San Briz
by Okudart**

Dob u. 4, Erzsébetváros

Throughout WWII, Spain remained neutral, granting its diplomats a special position. Angel San Briz was one of those diplomats and is often referred to as 'The Angel of Budapest'. He helped around 5,000 Hungarian Jews flee the country and certain death, by providing them with passports. His colourful portrait is to remind us all how much can depend on the kindness of others in troubled times.

**Sourdough can
be a bridge, too
by Viktória Hitka**

*Gerlóczy u. 6,
Erzsébetváros*

The Covid Pandemic struck Budapest just like any other city. The first lockdown made the streets go quiet, with tourists staying away and citizens staying indoors, not knowing what to do. And yet, it had one unexpected result: it seemed as though everyone became a baker. Suddenly, sourdough recipes were passed on, with tips on how to keep the starter alive, creating a warm bond and, a bridge between neighbours. The mural reminds us of community, and how it is good to slow down at times.

CINEMA

In Hungary international films are generally dubbed, which is why you need to be careful when choosing a film. You're likely safe when you find one with Hungarian subtitles, depending on the language of origin. Budapest, however, has some wonderful art cinemas to choose from.

Puskin

Kossuth Lajos u. 18, Belváros, puskinmozi.hu

You might not even notice it on the busy street, but Puskin is one of the oldest film houses of the city. Step back in time and enjoy the cosy atmosphere in one of the smallest screening rooms in the country with only sixteen seats, or sit in style at the pillar-flanked, magnificent main screen under the neo-classical illuminated ceiling.

Uránia

Rákóczi út 21, Belváros, urania-nf.hu/en

National film theatre Uránia is home to many cultural events, not just film screenings, with its large stage in the main hall. The chandeliered screening room undoubtedly makes Uránia the most impressive cinema in Budapest, where a night at the cinema feels like going to the opera. Feel free to have a look around and sit down for a drink while you're there.

Művész

Teréz krt. 30, Andrássy út & Városliget, muveszmozi.hu

As the largest of all art cinemas, Művész has a balanced selection of popular films and independent movies. Its façade, with carved, totem-like pillars at the entrance, is instantly recognisable. Its proximity to tram lines 4 & 6, which run all night, means you don't have to worry about catching a late screening.

Bem Mozi

Margit krt. 5, Óbuda & Margaret Island, cooltix.hu/b/bemmozi

If you are looking for the most laid-back cinema experience, you shouldn't miss Bem Mozi. Although it is a small, independent cinema with just one screen, it is also a lively bar and offers the most diverse and extensive selection of non-Hungarian films, with hardly any of them dubbed. And even Hungarian films are subtitled in English. They show true cinema classics alongside new, international hits.

Cinema Mom

Alkotás u. 53, Buda Hills, cinemamom.hu

Don't let the fact that Cinema Mom is located on the top floor of a shopping centre discourage you. This is the place to be if you want to watch the latest blockbusters with very high-quality sound in the original language (often even without Hungarian subtitles). The large screening rooms are equipped with big comfy chairs and small tables to place your food and drinks on, and there's ample leg room for maximum comfort.

FESTIVALS

Budapest Spring Festival

Usually held at the end of April and early May, the Budapest Spring Festival offers a rich programme on over thirty locations, with dance, cinema, concerts, and exhibitions. This gives you the chance to explore parts of the city you might not visit otherwise.

budapestitavaszifesztival.hu/en

Tilos Maraton

Tilos Radio is one of the few remaining independent radio stations in the country, with music and opinions you might not hear in the mainstream media. A fundraising marathon event is held every first two weeks of June. With concerts, workshops for both children and adults and a traditional raffle.

tilos.hu

Kolorádó

Hidden in the woods of the Buda Hills, Kolorádó is a small, alternative festival. Chances are your mobile phone won't have any service here, so you can focus on the music. The lineup consists of local bands and performers, with some international headliners.

kolorado.hu

Sziget

Sziget means 'island' and the festival is held on Óbudai-sziget, 'Old Buda Island'. It is one of the largest in Europe, with over half a million visitors every August, mostly international, hence the pop-up embassies that provide instant help if needed. Big, international headliners, cultural activities, performances, dance, theatre, and workshops – Sziget has it all.

szigetfestival.com

Festival of Folk Arts

20th August marks St Stephen's day, Hungary's most important national holiday. It is celebrated with Europe's largest fireworks show in the evening. In the week leading up to the day, the Festival of Folk Arts is held at Buda Castle. Here, old crafts come to life again, with workshops, demonstrations, a market, concerts, and dance.

mestersegekunnepe.hu

BuSho International Short Film Festival

BuSho has been a significant part of Budapest's cultural scene for the past twenty years and is held annually in early September. They show films of young, independent filmmakers from Hungary and beyond, and the screenings are scattered around various cinemas and cultural institutions in the city.

bushofest.hu

Budapest Wine Festival

Hungary is proud of its excellent wine regions. This wine festival is usually held the second week of September, when hundreds of wineries come together in Buda Castle to display and sell their products. Some guest countries are present too, and there are two large stages with dance and music.

aborfesztival.hu

Inner City Beer Festival

Local breweries from Budapest and other parts of the country have sprouted over the past decade, with some very noteworthy creations. They all come together on Szabadság Square in early September. Entry to the festival is free of charge, but you have to buy your own beer glass to have your drinks served in.

sorfesztival.hu

THINGS TO DO

Buda Castle Cave Tour

Did you know that there's a whole labyrinth underneath Buda Castle? Actually, it is something that even many locals don't know. The Buda Castle Cave Tour takes you through these centuries-old cellars and allows you to discover a hidden part of the city. It is especially recommended in summer, when the cool temperature of the caves is very welcome.

1014, Dárda u. 2, Buda Castle, budacastlebudapest.com

Cycle tour with BudaBike

BudaBike tours will take you along the most important highlights of the city in 2.5 hours. They provide English, Dutch, German, and French language tours, as well as thematic tours on demand, and all gather in front of the Basilica. Want to explore the city on your own by bike? They also operate as a bike rental.

1051, Szent István tér 4, Belváros, budabike.com

Legenda Boat tour

A Danube cruise is a great way to explore the most prominent sights of the city. And what better way to do this than by night, over dinner? Legenda offers candle-lit boat tours with dinner at a fixed price, to enjoy Budapest by night from a different angle. You can also book a guided hour-long tour in the daytime with a complimentary drink. Guides are available in over thirty languages.

1052, Jane Haining rkp. 7, Belváros, legenda.hu

Thematic tours by Hosszúlépés

Hosszúlépés, meaning 'long step', is a pun referring to a type of *fröccsl*, a drink made from wine and sparkling water. They offer thematic cultural tours digging deeper into the secrets of Budapest and exploring the city from a different angle. Their 'Jewish Roots and Revival' tour is especially recommended, as it will give you a better insight into the Jewish district, now the main nightlife area of the city. They also offer several tours themed around the wonderful architectural treasures that Budapest offers.

1052, Kristóf tér 7-8, Belváros, hosszulepes.org

↓ BIKING NEAR BARTÓK BÉLA BOULEVARD

Thermal Baths

Thermal baths are an important feature of the city and of the Hungarian identity. It stems from a combination of excellent groundwater reserves that are naturally hot and full of important minerals (hence the sulphuric smell), and the 150 years of Ottoman occupation in the 16th and 17th centuries that brought bathhouse culture to Budapest. Water temperatures can vary between 30 and 40 degrees, which is why you should always read the user advice for any pool. The waters have beneficial properties for muscle and joint pains and rheumatic

symptoms. You can also indulge in extra services like a massage, the steam room or a mud bath.

spasbudapest.com

Ride along the Danube on tram 2

A ride along the Danube on tram 2 is one of the most fun, affordable ways to have a sightseeing trip. The tram runs on the Pest bank between Jászai Mari tér at the foot of Margaret Bridge, right until Közvágóhíd, at the foot of Rákóczi Bridge. On your journey on one of the most scenic tram rides of the world, you will pass sights like the Parliament Building, the Chain Bridge, and Széchenyi Square on the Pest side, while looking out onto the Castle District, the Castle Garden Bazár and Gellért Hill on the Buda side. If you don't have a lot of time in the city, this is the best way to make the most of your time.

bkk.hu/en/timetables

City Park Lake

The City Park offers a range of things to do to fill a full day, with the boating lake at its centre. In summer, you can rent a boat or SUP to cool off on a hot day at the foot of the Vajdahunyad Castle, whereas in winter it is turned into an ice-skating rink. The rink is even more magical in the evening, when the sights around it are lit.

1146, Olof Palme stny. 5, Városliget, csonakazoto.hu, mujegpalya.hu

Füvészkert

The Botanical Gardens of ELTE University are the largest and richest of its kind in the city. It has a wide variety of indigenous as well as exotic plants, and it is also a serene island of peace in a busy environment. From time to time, the botanical gardens serve as a venue for special events, such as concerts and exhibitions, and they often provide thematic programmes and tours around holidays.

1083, Illés u. 25, Józsefváros, fuveszkert.org

Flippermúzeum

If the day is rainy or you feel like you need a break from all the Budapest-related sights, it's time to hit the arcade! Even though it is called a museum, this pinball heaven has the largest collection of pinball machines in Europe – some of which of museum quality. And yet, everything is there to be used, even antique pieces from 1932! After paying an entrance fee, all machines are free to use, and you may exit and re-enter throughout the day using your wristband.

1137, Radnóti Miklós u. 18, flippermuzeum.hu

Elisabeth lookout

Once you're up in the Buda Hills, the one thing you mustn't miss out on is the Elisabeth lookout. The 528m tower on top of János Hill is the highest point of the city and grants you a breathtaking view of not only the surrounding landscape, but also the city itself. On a clear day, you can see all the way to the Tátra Mountains in Slovakia. Descend with the Zugliget Chairlift for a fun journey of around twelve minutes, covering a height of 262m.

Buda Hills, normafapark.hu, bkk.hu

Budapest Children's Railway

Another unique experience to try when you are in the Buda Hills is the Children's Railway. This service is run entirely by Scouts (under adult supervision) and has a longstanding tradition. On selected days, the train is pulled by a steam locomotive. You can take a return journey between Hűvösvölgy and Széchenyi-hegy or get off at selected stops that the train serves, such as Normafa or János-hegy.

Buda Hills, gyermekvasut.hu

FAMOUS PEOPLE

Hungary and Budapest have produced quite a few celebrities over the centuries, even though you may never have known about their roots. Sadly, this is often because many Hungarian families fled the country during WWII and in the aftermath of the revolution of 1956, setting up a new life elsewhere.

Zsa Zsa Gabor

Hungarian American Zsa Zsa was a quintessential celebrity, reigning over Hollywood from the 1950s. Known as an actress and all-round beautiful woman, she rose to fame with films like the 1952 *Moulin Rouge*, and she stayed in the limelight through her appearances in talk shows and interviews, impressing people with her quick wit and confidence.

Harry Houdini

Although he became the most famous escape artist the world has ever seen while living in the United States, Houdini was born in Budapest to a Hungarian family and moved across the pond as a child. He was born Erik Weisz but changed his name when he became a magician.

László Bíró

Bíró's legacy has in all likelihood left its mark on each and every one of our lives. While working as a journalist, he yearned for a way to use quick-drying ink in a pen, which ultimately led to his invention of the ballpoint pen. A common name for his invention borrows his name: biro.

Ernő Rubik

A professor of architecture turned toy inventor. Rubik invented a cube of which all individual parts could be moved around while keeping the internal structure intact. Give all parts on the outside different colours, and you've created the world-famous Rubik's cube! Even though it has over three billion possible combinations, it is always solvable within twenty moves. The current world record for solving the Rubik's cube is 3.13 seconds!

Robert Capa

Capa, born Endre Ernő Friedman, was a renowned Budapest-born photojournalist and a leader in the field of war and combat photography. He captured many conflicts in Europe and Asia throughout the 20th century and was even present on Omaha Beach on D-Day. He is also credited for coining the term Generation X. He ultimately got too close to the action: he died after stepping on a landmine in Vietnam.

George Soros

Soros is a Hungarian-born billionaire, who made his fortune on the stock market. He has a reputation for giving large amounts of money to civil rights groups and other philanthropic endeavours. However, his influence is often criticised in circles that admire strongman leadership.

Michael Curtiz

Born in Budapest, Curtiz became one of the most widely recognised film directors of Hollywood's Golden Age. He worked with and arguably launched the careers of of the likes of Bette Davis and Errol Flynn. Curtiz won an Academy Award for Best Director following his success with the cinema classic *Casablanca*.

Ferenc Puskás

Puskás is a legendary football player who was mostly known for his goal scoring prowess, winning three European Cups with Real Madrid, and reaching a World Cup final with Hungary's golden generation in the 1950s. The Puskás award, handed out for the best goal each year, was named after him. After his passing in 2006, he was buried in St. Stephen's Basilica.

Zoltán Kodály

Kodály was a classical composer who travelled around Hungarian lands to collect folk songs to incorporate in his music. His greatest legacy, however, might be the Kodály method for music pedagogy, and people travel to Hungary from all over the world to enhance their skills as music teachers for children.

Béla Bartók

Bartók is considered one of the most influential composers of the 20th century and is especially recognised for his work in analysing and collecting folk music, often being mentioned alongside Kodály, though perhaps more frequently as a singular influential figure.

Franz Liszt

Completing our short list of classical composers, Liszt is often considered Europe's very first popstar: the crowds went wild wherever he went. He grew up outside Hungary and spoke unintelligible Hungarian, but he was outspoken about his love for the country, nevertheless. This is reason enough for Hungarians to get into heated arguments with Austrians about who can claim Liszt as their own.

András Arató

If you have had access to the internet in the 2010s, there is a good chance you have seen the 'smile' of Arató, although more people are probably familiar with his nickname 'Hide the pain Harold'. Having become an internet sensation after his stock photos went viral, he will now often appear in adverts.

FILMS & SERIES IN AND ABOUT BUDAPEST

Although not a lot of Hungarian films make it to the international market and only a few can be found on Netflix, many are worth watching. Most Hungarian films are affordably available for streaming with English subtitles via *filmio.hu*, and you can find the more recent ones on *cinego.hu*.

Budapest (2018)

This French comedy tells the story of two friends who decide to quit their boring jobs to become stag party planners in Budapest. As the parties get wilder, the audience gets a good feel of the nightlife of the city that is indeed a popular destination for stag parties and hen dos.

Red Sparrow (2018)

This is one of the few blockbusters not only filmed but also set in Budapest, starring Jennifer Lawrence as an elite Russian spy, a Sparrow. Her character, a prima ballerina, is trained to become a perfect, seductive killing machine, tasked to infiltrate the CIA to find the mole within the Russian intelligence services. And so, she sets off to Budapest to fulfil her mission.

I Spy (2002)

Another classic, with Eddie Murphy and Owen Wilson, based on the 1960s television show of the same name. A spy and a boxer travel to Budapest to prevent a secret weapons deal, selling to the highest bidder. The film could just as well be a promotional video for the city, with spectacular shots of the skyline and main highlights.

Semmelweis (2023)

This film dramatizes the remarkable story of Ignaz Semmelweis, the physician who hypothesised that washing your hands before engaging in obstetrics could save a lot of mothers' lives. And knowing what we know now, he was right.

Lefkovichék gyászolnak (All about the Lefkoviches, 2024)

This feelgood film takes you through the complex process of dealing with loss through the eyes of three generations: grandfather, father, and son. Even though it is a heavy topic, the film has a lot of wit and is sure to make you both cry and laugh.

Van valami furcsa és megmagyarázhatatlan (For some inexplicable reason, 2014)

In this debut of lauded director Gábor Reisz, you get a sense of the inescapable melancholy many Millennials associate with being Hungarian. Set in the city, it offers a genuine glimpse into the life of an average Budapester.

Rossz versek (Bad poems, 2018)

With his masterful irony, Gábor Reisz draws a parallel between a broken heart and a broken society. Heavy as that sounds, you can sit back and enjoy as the serene images of Budapest float by, accompanied by a lovely soundtrack, and experience what it means to live in the city.

Magyarázat mindenre (Explanation for everything, 2023)

In this award-winning film, Gábor Reisz chillingly captures the dysfunctional and polarising way in which contemporary politics are discussed in Hungarian homes, and the consequences this has in the public sphere.

Kontroll (2003)

Get underground with this iconic film noir, portraying the comings and goings of the ticket inspectors of the Budapest transport system.

Moszkva tér (2001)

Although it is now called Széll Kálmán tér, many still call it by its old name, Moszkva tér (Moscow Square). In the 1990s, it used to be the quintessential meeting point for young people, a sentiment that this film captures for eternity.

A tanú (The Witness, 1969)

A cult classic among Hungarians, this film was at one point banned from being screened for its criticism of the favouritism and theatrics within the communist regime. The protagonist, by all means a simple man, becomes the key witness in a highly politicised trial. In this film, the absurdity of show trials is laid bare. A very quotable film as well, for those with an interest in learning Hungarian.

Szabadság, szerelem!
(Children of Glory, 2006)

This dramatized version of the events of the 1956 Revolution will give you an action- and romance-filled insight into this segment of Hungarian history.

Most vagy soha!
(Now or never!, 2024)

This film's title was taken from one of the poems of Sándor Petőfi, hero of the uprising in 1948, and follows the dramatized events of 15th March as seen through his eyes. Produced with one of the largest budgets in Hungarian film history, it is a visual delight.

BOOKS IN & ABOUT BUDAPEST

Sorstalanság (Fatelessness) – Imre Kertész

This Nobel Prize-winning work tells the story of a fifteen-year-old surviving Auschwitz and Buchenwald, the horrors of the concentration camp, and life after death and destruction. The novel was adapted into a film bearing the same title.

A Pál utcai fiúk (The Paul Street Boys) – Ferenc Molnár

Classic Hungarian literature and a must-read for all schoolchildren growing up in the country. Paul Street is located in Józsefváros, and the statue of playing boys in that street underscores the novel's cultural significance. The book is about friendship, standing up for what is right, and about being a boy in Budapest in the first half of the 20th century.

Budapest Noir – Vilmos Kondor

Published in multiple countries and languages, Budapest Noir is the first of a five-part crime series set in the Hungarian capital. The detective story revolves around the body of a young woman found in the streets of Budapest in 1936, and it is up to a young journalist to unfold the mystery.

Budapest Noir: Ilona gets a phone – Alison Langley

Confusingly sharing part of its title with Kondor's bestseller, this debut novel by Irish American novelist Alison Langley focuses on 1990s Budapest and the fall of the Iron Curtain, where protagonist Ilona looks forward to a bright new future, although the socialist past still lingers.

Narratives of Budapest – essay collection

With this recent collaboration between writers, journalists, local historians, and other remarkable figures of contemporary Budapest, you can dive into a colourful picture of the city, as seen from a multitude of perspectives. This allows you to not only discover the past and present of Budapest but also follow the evolving narrative of its citizens.

Budapest – Viktor Sebestyén

Sebestyén tells the full history of Budapest without being long-winded. From famous events to famous people, and how they are all interwoven with the broader history of Hungary, this book will leave you feeling like an expert after finishing a readthrough.

Twelve Days – Viktor Sebestyén

This book offers a retelling of the massive fateful Hungarian revolt in 1956, starting with the broader context and eventually going through all the events of the rebellion as if it were a gipping thriller. While reading, you might forget that the moments described are, sadly, not fictional.

Tainted Democracy – Zsuzsa Szelényi

Szelényi was once an important member of Fidesz, the now-ruling political party that started as a movement for young liberals. Nowadays, it is widely accepted that the party has eroded Hungarian democracy, and this book by Szelényi details how this happened.

The Picnic – Matthew Longo

Even though Hungary nowadays is great at building fences on its borders, in 1989 it was Hungary that made the first breaches into the Iron Curtain that brought the fall of the Berlin Wall, with ... a party! This book gives a great overview of how East Germans fled to West Germany aided by and travelling through Hungary through and, for which Longo received the Orwell Prize for Political Writing.

Strangers in Budapest – Jessica Keener

When a young American couple moves from Boston to Budapest after the fall of the Communist regime, they don't know that a call for help will upend their lives, tracking down the son-in-law of a WWII veteran that supposedly killed his daughter. Embarking on this manhunt uncovers more than they bargained for ...

Macskakő (Cobblestone) – Péter Lengyel

If you haven't fallen in love with Budapest yet, you will after reading this remarkable novel. Starting with seemingly unrelated scenes set in the city, the novel gradually reveals how everything is interconnected, by the end leaving you with a vivid sense of the city's cobblestones beneath your feet.

FUN FACTS

The lions of the Chain Bridge

Most remarkable on the Chain Bridge, the first permanent bridge connecting Buda and Pest, are the four lions standing guard at both ends. They are also subject to what is probably the most popular urban legend of the city. It is said that the sculptor, when boasting about his commission in a drunken mood, made a wager that his lions would be without flaw. Upon completion, one of his pub-mates pointed out that the stone animals appeared to have no tongues. Driven by the shame this had caused him, the artist jumped into the Danube from the very bridge for which he had created the lions.

Story of St. Margaret

Princess Margaret of Hungary was the 8th and youngest daughter of King Béla IV. When she was born, Mongols roamed the land, and the royals had to evacuate to Croatia. The king vowed that if God liberated the land from its enemy, he would dedicate his daughter to the church. At the age of six, she was moved into the monastery on Nyulak Szigete (Island of Rabbits), where she spent the rest of her dedicated life, having refused many an arranged political marriage. The island, as you may have guessed, was subsequently renamed in her honour: Margaret Island.

Story of St. Gellért

Saint Gellért (Gerard) was a bishop in early 11th-century Hungary. He settled in the country during its conversion to Christianity, serving as tutor to

FUN FACTS

the son of King Stephen I. He truly became a legend for his martyrdom, though, for which several accounts exist. The most widely accepted story is of him being put in a barrel by pagans during a revolt and rolled down what is now known as Gellért Hill.

How Ferenc Molnár threw away the key to Café New York

Budapest had a buzzing literary scene in the 19th and 20th centuries, whose members frequented various cafés and pubs around the city. Most popular was Café New York, part of an exquisite hotel. Novelist Ferenc Molnár was a regular there; he even wrote most of *The Paul Street Boys* at one of its tables. Legend has it that one evening, the merry patrons of the establishment decided it should be open day and night, so a group of them, led by Molnár, simply took the key to the front door and threw it into the Danube. Whether this really happened, nobody knows, but it adds a bit of colour to the café's history.

Dating at Gerbaud

Another popular legend is related to the upper-class confectionery and café on Vörösmarty Square: Gerbaud. In the 19th and early 20th centuries, it used to be one of few co-ed public spaces, which meant that members of both sexes could meet there and get to know each other. However, legend has it that this was also the hunting ground of wealthy ladies for younger lads up for some fun. Apparently, an elaborate system of signals was in place, based on what was ordered — someone's interest could be indicated by the combination of a specific cake and sparkling water, or a strategically placed spoon, with the number of sugar cubes stacked next to the cup as a price indication.

Kolodko statues

Anyone with a keen eye can find small sculptures scattered around Budapest, mostly in places where people walk by unaware. They are all made by Mihály Kolodko, and they often reference their location or to the history of Hungary itself, such as a Rubik's cube by the Danube or a moon buggy on Hold utca, Moon Street (both designed by a Hungarian).

Filming locations for big productions

Second only to London, Budapest is a major European filming location, attracting even Hollywood productions. Because the scenery in many of Budapest's streets could potentially evoke any beautiful European city, even films set in Paris or Russia will often be shot in Budapest. Madonna, for example, sang *Don't Cry for Me Argentina* from the balcony of the Opera house. It is therefore not unusual to find entire streets cordoned off and filled with production lorries, or to see French street signs obscuring the Hungarian originals. And if you encounter a tank while strolling about, it's likely there for a war movie.

Oldest underground of mainland Europe

It runs for the largest part under the Andrássy Boulevard and Városliget, between Vörösmarty tér and Mexikói út – but did you know that metro line M1 is the oldest underground railway in mainland Europe? Only preceded by the London Underground, this popular transport route is still as glorious as it was at its opening in 1896 – in time for the Millennium celebrations. Despite undergoing some renovations over the years, it remains a sight to behold, as recognised by UNESCO in 2002.

PHOTO SPOTS

The Parliament Building from Batthyány tér

Some say the best thing about Pest is the view of beautiful Buda. However, for the best shot of the Parliament Building, you do need to be on the other side of the Danube. This spot is particularly magical when the full moon rises right behind the majestic building.

Sunrise at Fisherman's Bastion

If you can, catching the sunrise between the pillars of the deserted Fisherman's Bastion during the quiet morning hours is a must. The golden rays on the white marble are worth the early start.

City panorama #1: Top of Gellért Hill

It makes sense to take the high ground for a panorama shot — when climbing up to the Citadel, take the north side, where the trees are cleared for the best view of the Danube, Buda Castle, and the Pest side.

City panorama #2: Philosophers' Garden

For the most romantic cityscape, take a photo of the statue of the Princess of Pest and the Prince of Buda holding hands, with the city in the background. The bond of the two lovers symbolises the joining of what were once two cities.

↓ ST. STEPHEN'S

↓ PHILOSOPHER'S GARDEN

Danube panorama: Liberty Bridge

The unmistakable green curves of Szabadság-híd, Liberty Bridge, run between Szent Gellért tér on the Buda side and Fővám tér on the Pest bank. Apart from it granting a nice view of the river, Gellért Hill, and Buda Castle, the bridge is also a popular place to sit on and enjoy a pleasant evening with a drink or a slice of pizza. Some make the effort to bring a picnic blanket with glasses and a bottle of wine.

City centre panorama: 360 Bar

Rooftop bars are always a great way to rise above the city, take in the view, and enjoy a nice drink to go with it. 360 Bar is located right in the centre of Budapest, and therefore offers a breathtaking panorama all around, with the Buda Hills on one side, and the sprawling Pest side on the other. As Budapest has always had a strict building policy, there are no skyscrapers to destroy the view, so on a clear day you might see as far as the Tatra Mountains in the north.

Danube boat tour

If you're looking for a different angle, how about shooting from the Danube? You can get quite close to the Parliament building, and your panoramic shots of the Buda side are unobstructed by wires or other barriers. Doing the boat tour at night gives the pictures a bit of extra glamour.

Chain Bridge & Buda Castle	Széchenyi tér is where the Chain Bridge begins on the Pest side. It is essentially a large roundabout, and standing in the centre offers the perfect shot of the bridge with Buda Castle in the background. If you feel very daring, you can even stand on the little concrete island that separates the two road lanes, at the foot of the bridge.
City panorama 3: Centre of Margaret Bridge	To recreate the iconic shot from the film *Bad Poems*, you'll need to position yourself in the centre of Margaret Bridge, on the southern side. At this point, the Danube is at its broadest, which is why you'll get an almost full panorama of all the sights, including the Parliament Building, Gellért Hill, Buda Castle with the Fisherman's Bastion, and the Buda Hills in the background.
Basilica	The stunning Neo-Gothic building of the Basilica is hard to capture, as it is massive. The best way to go about it is to walk down Zrínyi Street towards the Danube. Turn around at the corner of Nádor Street and take in the cathedral in all its splendour, nicely framed by the buildings along the street.

↓ CITY PANORAMA #1

PHOTO SPOTS

BAKERIES

Pékműhely

pekmuhely.hu

'All you need to make good bread is high quality flour, water, salt, and sourdough' This is Pékműhely's motto, and based on how popular they are, they're on to something! If nothing else, you should try their signature whole-grain *kakaóscsiga*, a chocolate snail pastry. You can find them on two locations in the Buda Castle District and Újbuda.

Három Tarka Macska

haromtarkamacska.hu

With three outlets in Budapest, this artisan bakery has a wide selection of breads, both sweet and savoury pastries, and sandwiches. Their croissants, based on a traditional French recipe, are absolutely divine. Their name comes from a popular nursery rhyme about three cats in a mill.

Arán Bakery

aranbakery.hu

Arán means 'bread' in Irish, and behind this venture lies the remarkable story of a young Hungarian couple that moved to Dublin to try their luck. Working in hospitality and later studying the art of pastry and bread making, they decided to bring the art of baking back to their homeland, winning prizes such as Best Sourdough and Best Fermented Product. They have two shops, one in Belváros and one in Újbuda.

Tibidabo

1074, Dohány u. 7, Belváros, tibidabopekseg.hu

Budapest is a great city for people with dietary needs, as many places offer gluten-, lactose- or sugar-free options. If you want to be completely safe, go to Tibidabo. Not only is everything guaranteed gluten-free, there is also a great variety of cakes, pastries, and sandwiches, as well as hot and cold drinks, to have in or take away. There is a large office space upstairs.

Butter Brothers

1093, Lónyai u. 22, Ferencváros, butter-brothers.com

Butter Brothers is not only a bakery, but also a bistro with a soup of the day and on weekdays great sandwiches for a quick lunch. You must try their *kalács* for breakfast – a sweet, braided bread that goes really well with butter and jam. They are closed on Sundays.

Manfréd

1094, Tompa u. 21, Ferencváros, fb @manfredpekseg

When roaming around Ferencváros, this is an excellent stop to get a nice cold drink in summer or a hot one to warm up, accompanied by one of the delicious sweet or savoury pastries and cakes. Their *bejgli*, a traditional Christmas delicacy with walnut or poppy seeds, is especially recommended.

BREAKFAST & BRUNCH

Franziska

franziska.hu

With a range of healthy vegetarian, vegan, and gluten-free options, all-day breakfast, and delicious cakes, Franziska is an excellent choice for brunch or lunch. The portions are large and filling, and with its laid-back ambience, this place is a real treat. With two locations in the city, the one in Belváros is worth booking a table for, as it can get very busy.

Szimply

1052, Károly krt. 22, Belváros,
insta @szimplyfood

Hidden in a small arcade (Röser udvar), this little all-day brunch venue will add colour to your day. With sweet and savoury bowls, bagels, and egg-variations, accompanied with self-roasted specialty coffees, you cannot go wrong by choosing to stop by. The composition of the dishes is highly Instagrammable.

Zoska

1053, Ferenczy István u. 28, Belváros, zoska.hu

Breakfast is the most important meal of the day, which is why you can enjoy it all day long at Zoska, even if you get up late. Take a seat in a comfy chair, and take your time waking up while the smell of food and fresh coffee surrounds you. Don't forget to leave a Post-it note on the wall to join the breakfast lovers before you.

Grumpy

1072, Klauzál u. 34, Belváros,
grumpybudapest.hu

Whether you're grumpy before your first coffee or ready for a break after a busy morning, Grumpy is the place to recharge. Apart from the usual breakfast options, their all-day brunch menu includes superfood options, and you can try a typical Hungarian delicacy: sausages made from *mangalica*, a unique Hungarian pig breed often called the 'sheep pig'. They also have a range of salads, French-style lunch options, and main courses inspired by international cuisine.

Anyám szerint

1077, Wesselényi u. 25, Belváros, anyamszerint.hu

What does breakfast look like, according to your mum? That's the question Anyám szerint tries to answer, with its homely decor and excellent choices for breakfast and lunch. They have a wide range of vegan and gluten-free options, and traditional Hungarian as well as more contemporary items. In summer, their hidden garden is the best place to chill.

Cirkusz

1074, Dob u. 25, Belváros, cirkuszbp.hu

With its unique interior and excellent kitchen, Cirkusz is a popular brunch spot with locals and visitors alike. That is why booking a table is always highly recommended. You can now also buy their specialty coffee beans, winner of several barista prizes.

Tompa17

1094, Tompa u. 17/a, Ferencváros, fb @tompa17

A true living-room vibe to start or end your day. Breakfast is served until noon, after which you can choose from their range of *challah* sandwiches, soup or tapas, accompanied by some bubbles or one of their excellent Hungarian wines.

LUNCH

Hungarians usually eat a hot meal for lunch, which is why many places offer lunch deals of two or three courses: a soup, a main, and sometimes a dessert. These offers usually apply on weekdays only, when office workers go out to have lunch during their break. To avoid the crowds, it's best to time your lunch after 1pm.

Zërgë & Wombät

1011, Fő u. 7, Buda Castle District; 1114, Bartók Béla út 37

Bagels and coffee, a combination for the ages. You don't really need much more for a quick lunch, and at the twin venues of Zërgë and Wombät, you'll be in great hands. The owners are fond of alternative metal music, which you'll notice in some interior design features and their choice of background music.

Kelet

1114, Bartók Béla út 29, Újbuda, keletkavezo.hu

Situated on the buzzing, cultural hub that is Bartók Béla Boulevard, Kelet is a popular choice for many locals to hang

out. With a monthly changing menu that always features two soups, two mains, and some salads and sandwiches, it's a simple but delicious option for lunch (or even dinner). The coffee is excellent, and their homemade coffee ice-cream affogato is a must-try in summer.

Műhely Egyetem Café

1088, Múzeum krt. 4/a, Belváros, insta @muhelycafe

There is nothing more authentic than to mingle with local students. And the students of ELTE University are very lucky to have Műhely on their campus: this is a café that deserves a much more prominent location. With a soup of the day, a daily changing vegetarian and meat-based dish, a wide range of tasty sandwiches, raw vegan cakes, salads, and puddings, and of course excellent coffee, it would be worth going back to school.

Fecske Presszó

1088, Baross u. 10, fecskepresszo.hu

Fecske is popular among students for their affordable lunch menu or just a drink. Apart from the daily changing soup-and-main combination, they also have a menu to choose from. If there are no free tables outside, there is a rather large indoor area in the basement where you can take a seat.

Lumen

1085, Horánszky u. 5, lumen.hu

Based in an arts centre, Lumen has a bright, minimalistic interior, turned into a calm oasis by the multitude of plants. On weekdays, they also serve a two-course lunch menu, and their selection of tapas and attractive main courses are available the whole day. The hidden courtyard is a delightful addition to the industrial vibe.

Tosti

1055, Bajcsy-Zsilinszky út 76, Belváros, insta @tostibudapest

If there's one nation that has perfected toasties to a national dish, it's the Dutch. It's no wonder that Tosti serves the best in Hungary: Dutch-born Julika and Cédric have opened their small business in Budapest after the Covid-19 pandemic, and they're still going strong. This is also where you want to be if you are looking for no-nonsense coffee.

Hokedli

1065, Nagymező u. 10, Andrássy út & Városliget, fb @hokedli

Traditional Hungarian food is rich in fat, meat and carbs, so a vegan lifestyle has not traditionally been a natural fit for them. Hokedli was one of the first lunch establishments that served hot vegan and gluten-free alternatives. With their heart and soul poured into their cosy shop, it's nourishing for body and soul.

Csiga

1084, Vásár u. 2, Józsefváros, fb @cafecsiga

When you enter Csiga, you will immediately feel at home, with the wooden spiral staircase leading to the upstairs gallery, the high ceilings and plants, the enjoyable music, and the friendly people that are drawn in by the bohemian atmosphere. You can go for the daily lunch menu, and after lunchtime for the regular options.

Dagoba

1083, Práter u. 59, Józsefváros

Dagoba cuts straight to the point: they specialise in lunch, and lunch only, which is why they are only opened until 2pm. Being this specific allows them to really put all their efforts into their creations. These change daily and are based on seasonal vegetables

as well as their inspiration on the day. You can come in for a soup, at least two types of mains (one vegetarian), quiche, and sweet bites. A holistic lunch to fill you up for the day!

Jedermann

1092, Ráday u. 58, Ferencváros, fb @jedermann.budapest

Whenever you are in the neighbourhood, Jedermann is a good option – for breakfast, lunch (weekly menu), dinner, or just for a drink late at night. There is a good chance a jazz concert will be taking place, in which case you may have to buy a ticket. The dark and cosy interior has true smoky bar vibes – but smokers will be asked to proceed to the inner courtyard at the back.

STREET FOOD & SNACKS

Karaván Street Food Court

1075, Kazinczy u. 18, Belváros, insta @karavan_budapest

Travelling in a group of people who have different food preferences? Or are you food truck lovers? At this spot in the middle of the Jewish Quarter, a number of different food trucks are parked together. There are plenty of tables to sit at as well, but do note that it's entirely outdoors.

Lángos Papi

1075, Madách Imre út 3, Belváros

One of the best places to get Hungary's famed street food, the *lángos*. Fried doughy goodness, traditionally topped with garlic oil, sour cream, and cheese (more toppings are available, but some Hungarians consider adding extra toppings to be sacrilegious). Note that there is not much space to sit, so consider having one to take away.

PASTA.

1053, Kálvin tér 2, Belváros, fb @pastapont

The perfect, hearty street food for pasta lovers. Choose from a daily changing range of pastas, both classic recipes and inspired by international cuisine, and order a take-away to eat by the Danube or in the garden of the National Museum. Bear in mind that the venue is cash-only!

Molnár's kürtőskalács

1052, Váci u. 31, Belváros, kurtoskalacs.com

One of the most popular street foods to try in Hungary is the chimney cake. These tubular cakes, often coated with cinnamon, can be unravelled in a spiral. It's possible to get them with ice cream or other fillings, and although that may look appetising on pictures, be aware this could make your cake soggy and sticky.

Pizzica

1065, Nagymező u. 21, Andrássy út & Városliget, insta @pizzica_pizza

Pizza sliced into squares with a pair of scissors. Your average Italian would probably run away screaming, but that's how they roll at Pizzica – and who are we to argue, as the result is delicious.

Central market hall

1093, Vámház krt. 1-3, Ferencváros, piaconline.hu

It might seem obvious to say that you can get lunch at a market, but apart from the fact that you can indeed find all your groceries here, on the top floor you will find a wide selection of lunch options, from *lángos* to goulash and *pörkölt*, as well as fried sausages and pickled vegetables. A true Hungarian street-food vibe!

CUKRÁSZDA (CAKES & COFFEE HOUSES)

An important feature of Hungarian culture is a remnant of the Habsburg-era: the *cukrászda*, or confectioneries. Sitting down for cake and a coffee is not just for special occasions but is something you could do on a daily basis, or just to meet with friends or for a business meeting.

Ruszwurm

1014, Szentháromság u. 7, Buda Castle District, ruszwurm.hu

In Budapest you never have to walk far for cake. If you happen to find yourself near the Fisherman's Bastion or elsewhere in the Buda Castle District and are in dire need of *Eszterházy* cake or *Dobos* torta, may we suggest you stop by Ruszwurm? It has been there since 1827!

Asztalka

1013, Döbrentei u. 15, Buda Castle District, asztalkacukraszda.hu

Downhill from Buda Castle to the right of the church, Asztalka gives you that living-room feeling, the living room of a doll's house that is, with porcelain cups and saucers, silver spoons, and crocheted tablecloths. A real hidden gem!

Auguszt

1053, Kossuth Lajos u. 14-16, Belváros, auguszt.hu

The name Auguszt has graced the Hungarian coffeehouse scene for over 150 years, and they pride themselves on the quality of their baked goods, serving traditional Hungarian cakes and the savoury *pogácsa* – a small scone-type bake. Their venue in the city centre renders the Habsburg-vibe best, with a massive chandelier hanging from the ceiling.

↓ BÁLNA (SEE PAGE 133)

Hisztéria

1061, Andrássy út 44, Belváros, hiszteria.hu

The first branch of Hisztéria opened in the small town of Tápiószecső. The rest, as they say, is history. By now they are a household name in cakes and ice creams, and you can find their sweet treats in many cafés around the country. However, nothing beats getting it straight from the source: at one of their own shops.

Szamos

1052, Váci u. 1, Belváros, szamos.hu

As experts of chocolate, cakes, and marzipan, each Szamos franchise offers a nice place for a coffee break, and a good opportunity to find chocolaty presents for your friends back home. This specific location stands out by the richly decorated interior. As an added bonus, not many know about it, meaning you won't have to fight for an available table.

Dynamo Bake

1053, Képíró u. 6, Belváros, dynamobake.com

Whether you want to rent a bike immediately after your sugar intake, or you just want the enjoyment of a treat, dynamo has you covered. In this bakery-bike-rental hybrid, the ever so friendly staff are more than ready to assist, no matter which option you choose.

Nándori Cukrászda

1092, Ráday u. 53, Ferencváros, nandori.hu

While most of Ráday street is bustling, not many tourists venture to its far end, where they would be rewarded by the delicacies of Nádori. They have all the 'obligatory' cakes, as well as some signature sweet treats, such as the French salted caramel, and their chocolate-chestnut cake.

DINNER

ODA Bistro

1014, Czakó u. 15, Buda Castle District, odavagyunk.hu

Hidden behind a stone wall, you will find a little piece of the countryside. Within Czakó kert, ODA's fusion kitchen offers breakfast, lunch, and light dinners. Choose from fried goods, a range of pizzas and soups (also ramen), or order a platter to share. Whatever you choose, the quality of the ingredients is excellent.

Dobrumba / Marumba / Pingrumba

dobrumba.hu

It all started with Dobrumba, as a way to bring the mezze-focused Middle Eastern cuisine to Budapest. It became a massive success. Now, with Pingrumba focusing on specialities from

FOOD AND DRINKS

Cairo to Calcutta, and Marumba reinventing Hungarian cuisine, you have all the more options to choose from.

Mazel Tov

1073, Akácfa u. 47, Belváros, mazeltov.hu

At the ever so popular Mazel Tov, it is almost impossible to get a table without a booking. With its rustic interior, it would by all means qualify as a ruin bar (see page xxx), if it weren't a restaurant. The menu is largely based on Middle Eastern/Israeli cuisine, with mezzes, soups, and grilled bits, as well as hummus variations.

Kőleves

1075, Kazinczy u. 37-41, Belváros, kolevesvendeglo.hu

This restaurant with ruin garden gives the best value for money in the neighbourhood. The seasonally changing menu has a good selection of soups and mains, with vegetarian options. With the spacious, atmospheric interior, it's a nice spot to spend your evening.

Grinzingi

1053, Veres Pálné u. 10, Belváros, grinzingi.hu

Another odd one out, Grinzingi was designed in the image of Austrian brasseries from bygone times. However, their menu is what you would expect in a Hungarian restaurant. If you're there for a drink, try the *zsíros kenyér* – a slice of bread with goose fat and onion. A real delicacy!

Arquitecto Pitpit

1088, Ötpacsirta u. 2, Belváros, pitpit.hu

Located in the beautiful building that houses the Association of Hungarian Architects, this modern tapas and cocktail bar has everything you'd expect, plus a magical courtyard open during the peak season. The ivy-covered walls lit with fairy lights create a unique experience.

Szlovák étterem

1055, Bihari János u. 17, Belváros, bym.hu

If you wonder why we would recommend a Slovak restaurant in Budapest, one could argue that Slovak and Hungarian culture are intertwined, and that dishes like *sztrapacska*, a type of dumplings, might also be considered a Hungarian speciality. They offer the best *sztrapacska*, in many variations. And they also have a large selection of Hungarian items on the menu. Try their *Jókai bableves*, a hearty bean soup.

Karcsi Vendéglő

1066, Jókai u. 20, Belváros, karcsibacivendeglo.com

If you want to eat like the locals in a traditional Hungarian restaurant, without feeling overcharged because you're a tourist, try Karcsi. It is anything but fancy or glamorous, but the food is good, the prices reasonable, and the lack of groups of tourists is guaranteed.

Szilvakék Paradicsom

1136, Pannónia u. 5, szilvakekparadicsom.hu

A good, traditional, Hungarian restaurant of the old-fashioned kind, with waiters that open your door and have learned their profession at a dedicated school. The food is excellent, especially their chicken soup; though everything on the menu is worth trying. In summer, they also serve outside, on the terrace.

Pozsonyi Kisvendéglő

1137, Radnóti Miklós u. 38, pozsonyi-kisvendeglo.eatbu.com

Traditional Hungarian restaurants have one thing in common: big plates of hearty food, ensuring no one leaves hungry. Pozsonyi is a terrific option for those who want to experience a more authentic way of dining in Hungary and avoid tourist traps.

BRING THE PARENTS

Twentysix

1061, Király u. 26, Belváros, twentysixbudapest.com

You can find Twentysix in the heart of the city, in what was once the inner courtyard of a building. Its distinguished look comes from living plants that reach up to the glass ceiling. Not only is the venue itself exquisite, but the food, which is influenced by Middle Eastern cuisine, is as well. And you can enjoy one of their signature cocktails to go with your meal. Booking in advance is a must.

KIOSK

1056, Március 15. tér 4, Belváros, kiosk-budapest.hu

This exciting venue in the heart of the city gives you a mix of Hungarian classics and daring bistro food. Eat à la carte or choose from the daily menu. The chefs at KIOSK manage to make seemingly dull items like potato *főzelék* (watery stew) into a fine dining delicacy. Don't forget to book a table.

Centrál Grand Café

1053, Károlyi u. 9, Belváros, centralgrandcafe.hu

Come to Centrál Grand Café for brunch, or just simply treat yourself to a filling breakfast fit for Habsburg Kings! A benedict heaven, with a variety of the egg dish on the menu, with also a large selection of other brunch options, including soups and various warm bites. Finish with a taster of typical Hungarian cakes, and you might as well go shopping for larger trousers ...

GOING OUT

RUIN PUBS & BEER

The Jewish district has a rich heritage, and most buildings are listed as monuments, which poses difficulties in renovation – not only in terms of permits but also in terms of cost. At the beginning of this century, pubs were opened in old, almost ruined buildings, as an opportunity to prevent them from 'going to waste' as the buildings wouldn't be restored to their former glory anyway. This is how ruin pubs were initially founded, starting with the now iconic Szimpla kert. Nowadays, they are an important cultural feature of the city's nightlife, as well as a clear example of how Hungarians can make the most of any situation.

Szimpla kert

1075, Kazinczy u. 14, Belváros, szimpla.hu

Simply the most widely known ruin pub, and for good reason. Everywhere you look in this place, you'll find something new to catch your eye. It can get crowded at night, while it's calmer during the day, especially right after they open at 2pm.

Kőleves kert

1075, Kazinczy u. 37-41, Belváros, kolevesvendeglo.hu

Opened only in the warmer months from 4pm, Kőleves

kert is our pick of colourful beer gardens right in the Jewish quarter. It can host many people, making it a great option for groups if the weather allows it (which it usually does).

Pótkulcs

1067, Csengery u. 65/b, Andrássy út & Városliget, fb @potkulcsbudapest

You might miss it if you don't know where to look. A cosy little garden just off the beaten track, Pótkulcs offers a nice informal atmosphere. It's also a popular spot for dining, and if you're lucky, your visit might even be accompanied by a band playing live music.

Füge udvar

1072, Klauzál u. 19, Belváros, fugeudvar.hu

You'd be forgiven for thinking you immediately know what this place has to offer as soon as you walk in and see the crowd of drinkers sharing large tables. However, if you take a walk downstairs, you'll discover an array of extra bars, bar games, and perhaps even a dancefloor.

Auróra

1084, Auróra u. 11, Józsefváros, auroraonline.hu

Probably the most alternative entry on this list, Auróra tends to draw a crowd from the young and urban underground and queer scene. With seating inside and outdoors, and frequent activities and concerts, guests rarely get bored. It's a very welcoming, open place where all are equal and free.

Rácskert

1072, Dob u. 40, Belváros, fb @racskert

Of the beer gardens in the Jewish Quarter, Rácskert is perhaps the best kept secret. It's not the largest option in the area, but when you're seated here with a drink in hand and food from a food truck – vegan options are often available – there's no reason not to put Rácskert on our list.

Lámpás

1074, Dob u. 15, Belváros, fb @lampaspub

An easy-to-miss venue if you're not paying close attention, as only the entrance is on ground level. Enter through the door and you'll immediately walk downstairs into a charming basement pub. There are often live performances on, attracting an 'underground' crowd in more ways than one.

CRAFT BEER

Mad House

1061, Anker köz 1-3, Belváros, madhousebudapest.hu

Mad Scientist is one of the largest craft breweries in Hungary, and at Mad House

↓ ÉLESZTŐ

they have a wide selection of their creations on tap. Located in the Jewish quarter, it also offers great food, so lovers of craft beer can easily spend a large part of their day here.

Monyó Tap House

1091, Kálvin tér 7, Belváros, monyo.hu

Monyó Brewery has their own pub, where you can taste most of their beers, as well as some guest brews. The pub itself has a friendly vibe, with swings at the bar for seating and an overall laid-back atmosphere.

Mélypont

1053, Magyar u. 23, Belváros, fb @melypont

Mélypont has a frequently changing offer of mainly local craft beers on tap, but maybe even more impressive is its whisky selection, of which the bartender is very proud. He's a real connoisseur and will gladly tell you all about the options if you catch him at quieter times.

Élesztő

1094, Tűzoltó u. 22, Ferencváros, elesztohaz.hu

Located in an old industrial building, Élesztő has over thirty craft beers on tap, from local breweries and a few international options as well, including alcohol-free and fruity beers. But there are other drinks options: there is a wine bar in the same courtyard, and some street food options.

Rizmajer

1085, József krt. 14, Józsefváros, rizmajersor.hu

Rizmajer is the largest brewery on Csepel Island, a district in South Budapest, with a venue in the city centre. It offers all one could expect from a craft beer joint: a wide selection of draught beers, a kitchen serving pub food like burgers and fries, and you can watch big football matches on the screens.

Legfelsőbb Beeróság

1074, Dohány u. 20, Belváros, beerosag.hu

With ten beers on tap and over a hundred others in the fridge, Legfelsőbb Beeróság boasts an impressive selection of local and international craft beers. They also have a bar-food menu that is mainly focused on hamburgers.

DRINKS

Kiadó kocsma

1061, Jókai tér 3, Belváros, fb @kiadokocsma

Step into this old-fashioned pub that is mostly frequented by students and members of the alternative scene and take a seat at one of the wooden tables. Order a *tubi szóda*, a mix of an Israeli herb liqueur and sparkling water, and let the everyday lives of young Budapesters wash over you.

Szatyor bár

1111, Bartók Béla út 36, Újbuda, szatyorbar.hu

Together, neighbouring bars Hadik and Szatyor are an important feature of Bartók Béla Boulevard, but if you're going for a drink in one of them, pick Szatyor. Its lively interior with murals, rocking horses and other strange and colourful objects hanging from the ceiling and the varied and creative drinks menu all contribute to an unforgettable evening.

Mitzi

1114, Bartók Béla út 1, fb @mitzibudapest

Whether for a coffee in the morning or a drink at night, Mitzi is a great choice. At night, there is often live music, and combined with the interior design and lighting, this creates a lively but intimate atmosphere. Their kitchen is open until quite late too, so even having a bite is an option.

Könyvtár Klub

1088, Múzeum krt. 4, Belváros,
konyvtarklub.hu

This bar is housed underneath the Eötvös Loránd University's Faculty of Humanities, so expect the crowds to be young and the drinks cheap. You can also play games here, and during the warmer months you can sit on their large terrace above ground.

Mikszáth tér (Kis Fecske, Kislumen, Tikos a Tilos)

1088, Mikszáth Kálmán tér 1-3, Belváros,
fecskepresszo.hu, lumenbudapest.hu,
fb @tilosatilosofficial

This charming little square in the city's palace district is surrounded by bars, ranging from old, tried and true, to modern, cool and trendy. There are large seating areas outside, so you're very likely to find a table at one of the establishments any time.

Bálna (Esetleg, EscoBar, Rombusz)

1093, Fővám tér 11-12, Ferencváros,
balnabudapest.hu

Bálna is the Hungarian word for 'whale' and it refers to the modern whale-shaped building along the Danube close to the Liberty Bridge. In the 'whale', you'll find a handful of trendy bars, all with outside areas with wonderful views over the river and the beautiful Buda side across it, perfect for enjoying the sunshine.

Kisüzem

1077, Kis Diófa u. 2, Belváros, fb @Kisuzem

Much like the tourists, many locals will visit the Jewish Quarter for a drink simply because opening hours here tend to go on until later. Kisüzem is one bar that's often full of life, and the vast majority of the people creating the lively atmosphere are locals.

Warmup Cocktail Bar

1072, Nagy Diófa u. 26, Belváros, warmupbudapest.hu

For those who are keen on trying new drinks and cocktails, we recommend Warmup. Their staff enjoys experimenting with the menu, but ordering off-menu is encouraged too. They excel at personalising drinks to suit your taste.

Csendes

1053, Ferenczy István u. 5, Belváros, fb @csendesvintagebar

Csendes offers a nice, eclectic ambience, decorated with a whole assembly of different stickers, sticky notes, dolls, bathtubs, and other quirky decorations. Even though *csendes* means 'quiet', it's usually quite busy.

Hintaló

1081, Bacsó Béla u. 15, Józsefváros, hintalobar.com

A most peculiar and seemingly chaotic venue filled with regulars who all know each other, giving it a very friendly and warm atmosphere. It can get crowded, so it's good to have a Plan B if you don't find a free table.

Macska

1084, Bérkocsis u. 23, fb @macska23

Another wonderful example of the alternative scene of Budapest. Macska is excellent for grabbing a drink and also has a daily vegan menu, in case you're still peckish. You can take your drink up to the gallery, where you can sit on comfy cushions.

CLUBS

Instant-Fogas

1073, Akácfa u. 51, Belváros, instant-fogas.hu

The most popular party venue in the heart of the Jewish District, adding to the ruin bar scene. Live concerts are often organised in the Instant-Fogas twins, as well as in Robot, the third (more rock/metal-orientated) sister.

After a concert has finished, the whole venue transforms into a series of dance floors and becomes one large party hub. An entrance fee applies.

Doboz

1072, Klauzál u. 10, Belváros, doboz.co.hu

With its iconic tree right in the middle of the large courtyard where visitors gather to have a smoke, ruin pub Doboz has been a central part of the party scene. With dance floors as well as theme parties, Doboz caters for all audiences in the heart of the city.

Morrison's 2

1055, Szent István krt. 11, Belváros, morrisons2.hu

The party hub for local and exchange students alike, Morrison's is a reliable club, where you can dance on seven dance floors every day of the week. And when you're done dancing, try their karaoke bar!

Ellátó

1075, Kazinczy u. 34, Belváros, fb @ellatohaz

With live concerts, DJ sets, and parties, Ellátó is another addition to the city's ruin bars. It's a smaller venue than its brothers, but that makes your night out all the more intimate. Free entry.

Stifler Ház

1074, Dob u. 19, Belváros, stiflerhaz.hu

A large hall with live DJs and some side rooms with different music styles. Stifler adopts an industrial aesthetic, but with good music and wonderful company, the mood is quickly set either way, and the party can continue well into the night.

AlterEgo

1066, Dessewffy u. 33, Belváros, alteregoclub.hu

The only real queer bar, featuring drag shows, theme parties, and a welcoming

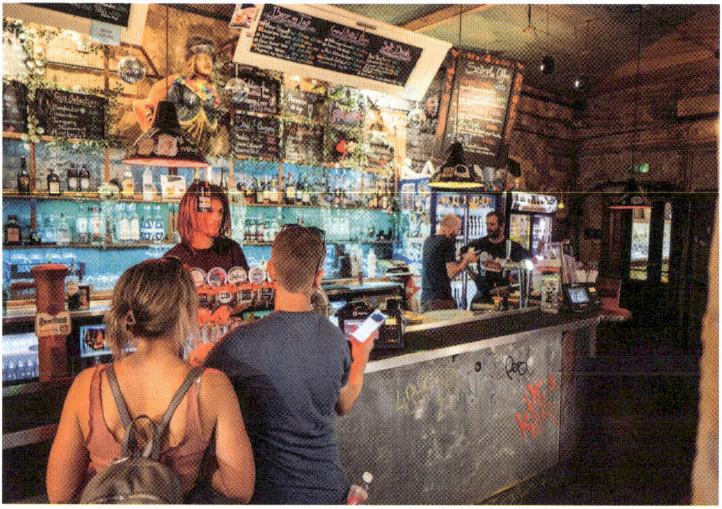

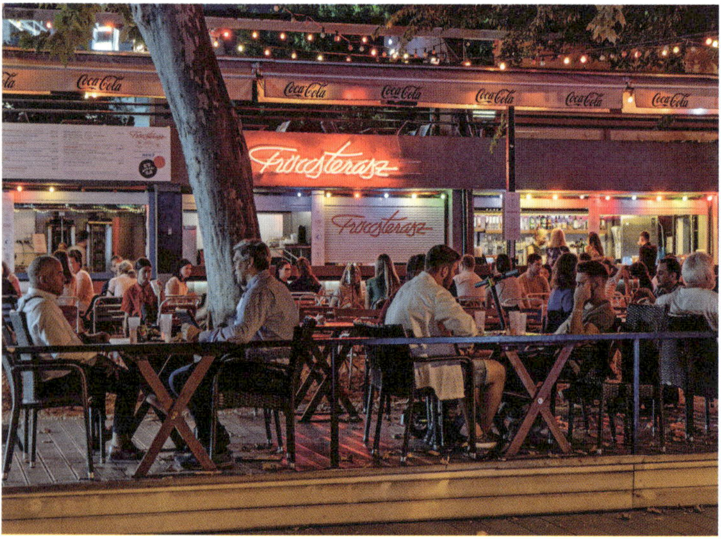
Coca-Cola
Coca-Cola
Coca-Cola
Coca-Cola
Coca-Cola
Coca-Cola

atmosphere to all. You can dance all night, sing karaoke or simply soak in the atmosphere. Only open on Friday and Saturday nights.

MUSIC VENUES

A38

1117, Petőfi híd, Újbuda, a38.hu

This concert and party venue is unique, not only because it is a boat, but also for its exceptional sound equipment, which guarantees a top-notch musical experience. In addition to hosting concerts across all genres, the venue hosts DJ sets and parties, either in the concert hall or on the deck. Don't miss the chance to party on a boat!

Dürer kert

1117, Öböl u. 1, Újbuda, durerkert.com

This cult venue popular among alternative locals has had to move from its majestic location next to Városliget, and has found another amazing venue along the Danube, so you can not only enjoy concerts inside but also can sit in the large outdoor area with a drink listening to one of the free concerts often held on the outdoor stage. They often host markets and small festivals too, such as Tilos maraton.

Fonó Budai Zeneház

1116, Sztregova u. 3, fono.hu

The place to go to for live Hungarian folk music from both the motherland and the diaspora, with dance houses and performances. And they often host guest countries, as well as artists from the world music scene.

Akvárium klub

1051, Erzsébet tér 12, akvariumklub.hu

This prestigious concert venue started out as the National Theatre's new location. After construction had started, the city government changed its minds about the location, and a large hole was left. This quickly filled with life as Gödör, which was later replaced by Akvárium. The square around it is a popular gathering place for young people to have a drink, play music or just chat.

Gödör

1061, Király u. 50, Belváros, godorunderground.hu

Literally meaning 'hole', Gödör moved from their actual hole in the ground to their new location in Király Street, where they continue to provide an important opportunity for members of the underground music scene to perform in front of an audience and build their following.

Turbina

1082, Vajdahunyad u. 4, Józsefváros, turbinabudapest.hu

Turbina is a popular party venue for young Budapesters with a taste for non-mainstream music and other artforms. A hipster hub where you can go to get your yearly fix of Club Mate.

Budapest Music Club

1093, Mátyás u. 8, Belváros, bmc.hu

For a more traditional approach to music, but still outside the classical genre, there is BMC. With a broad repertoire of jazz, world music, but also various other genres that don't fit conventional categories.

HOW TO DRESS LIKE A LOCAL

Being in Budapest is like being back in high school, where you can instantly recognise the 'cool kids', the metalheads, the alternative crowd, and the Barbie dolls. In short, you can be who you want to be, and dress accordingly. For budgetary as well as sustainable reasons, vintage clothes are very popular, and most young locals still have granny's post-socialist wardrobe to dive into. For those without, there is a wide range of shops to discover.

As summers tend to get very hot, it is normal for skirts and trousers to shorten as the days grow longer. By mid-July or August, aided by the festival season, don't be surprised to see bare-chested lads and girls in bikini tops walking in the street. Budapesters are very easy-going and won't think twice about going to the shops in their pyjamas if needed. On the other hand, a bourgeois generation still remains, and they would not be caught dead without always looking their best. However, everyone agrees that you need to put some effort into your outfit if you are going to a classical concert or to the theatre. Jeans are frowned upon on these occasions. And if you are planning to go to the opera – you may want to rent a ball gown or suit.

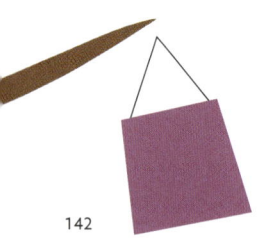

FLEA MARKETS, VINTAGE & SECOND-HAND

Dressing Room

1075, Síp u. 24, Belváros, insta @dressingroom2.0

Descend into a crazy boutique with carefully selected vintage and fun new items to add to your wardrobe. Their selection of wonderfully weird earrings is worth checking out, and they have a large range of denim jackets and trousers, both men's and women's.

Komondors Vintage Shop, Café & Bar

1077, Wesselényi u. 21, Belváros, insta @komondorsvintage

A *komondor* is a Hungarian sheepdog breed, as faithful to its owner as founding brothers Jordán and Jonatán are to sustainable fashion. Not only can you browse the high-quality items for sale, but you can also have a drink, and you might even catch a DJ set at night.

Gozsdu weekend market

1075, Gozsdu udvar, Belváros, gozsduudvar.hu, insta @gozsduweekend

Whether you arrive through Gozsdu Udvar via Király Street (number 13) or Dob Street (number 16), you will, on weekends, enter a buzzing set of arcades with stalls of various designer items and individuals selling their own antiques and miscellaneous objects. The market is open Fridays to Mondays, 10am to 5pm.

Szimpla market

1075, Kazinczy u. 14, Belváros, szimpla.hu

The most popular ruin pub of the city shows a very different side on Sunday mornings, when it turns into a farmer's market. Locals come to do their grocery shopping and find high-

FLEA MARKETS, VINTAGE & SECOND-HAND

quality products from rural Hungary. Every third Saturday of the month, the pub is opened for a design and crafts market, where local brands are on display with clothes, pottery, jewellery, and much more.

Ludovika

1075, Rumbach Sebestyén u. 15, Belváros, fb @ludovikashop

Specialised in vintage clothes for women, Ludovika prides itself on the carefully selected items of high quality. Apart from preloved clothes, they also stock upcycled pieces and some one-offs from their own workshop. Have a close look at their glass cabinets for unique jewellery made by local designers.

Retrock Designer Vintage Store

1061, Anker köz 2-4, Belváros, retrock.com

The largest of its kind, Retrock doesn't only stock vintage items, but also various designer brands from local makers. You can find some of their clothes in their web shop, but there's much, much more to be found in-store for men as well as women.

Szputnyik

1074, Dohány u. 20, Belváros, szputnyikshop.hu

Szputnyik started as a vintage shop but has evolved into a showroom for various local and international brands. With a large men's section on the top floor, you could just browse for hours. The rich selection of bags is worth checking out.

ReClaim Vintage

1077, Király u. 39,
Belváros,
insta @reclaimvintage.bp

At ReClaim Vintage, the emphasis lies on the shopping experience. With neatly displayed clothes and a good overview, this shop is not as overwhelming as some vintage shops can be. You can just browse comfortably and pick something from the selected items as if you were in a regular boutique.

Narancsliget

1075, Csányi u. 7,
Belváros,
fb @narancsliget.
adomanykozpont

Narancsliget functions primarily as a charity shop that collects donations for MAZS Foundation, founded by the American Jewish Joint Distribution Committee in 1991. The shop itself, however, is so much more than just a charity shop, with a special vintage department of selected items, from wedding dresses to retro bathing suits, from hats to fur coats: a happy collection of pre-loved items.

Budapest Royal Vintage

1074, Király u. 77,
Andrássy út & Városliget,
royalvintagebudapest.shop

Focusing on fashion items of the 80s and 90s, this shop has more of a retro vibe than that of a vintage shop. Yet, they have a reasonably priced selection of fun items to wear, even by big brand names like Adidas or Nike.

Jajcica

jajcica.hu

With two locations close to each other, you could easily spend a whole afternoon at Jajcica. They really have a bright, wonderful chaos of everything, from dresses to trousers to jackets and trainers. Their selection of shoes is extensive, categorised by brand, with many items from Converse, Vans, Timberland, and Dr Martens, but also with a large selection of tailor-made vintage shoes.

Lovebug Vintage / LoveChild Vintage

lovebugvintage.com

Step into the girly world of Lovebug and LoveChild Vintage, where everything may seem too pink and cute at first glance, but where you can find some real treasures, whether it be clothes, shoes or accessories. For Lovebug, you need to ring the doorbell to enter.

Konfekció

1086, József u. 16, Józsefváros, insta @konfekcio

The founder of Konfekció has one vision: to share her love for unique, 'old' clothes and show that anything can be fashionable. Therefore, she selects the items in her shop piece by piece, and you will definitely find some crazy Hungarian retro pieces here to take home with you, spreading the vintage love across borders.

Humana Vintage Astoria & Corvin

humanahasznaltruha.hu

Humana is a second-hand clothing chain with several shops where you can get dressed for very little money. Two of them are especially worth your while, as they are very good to go vintage treasure hunting: the ones at Corvin and Astoria. Both have a women's and men's section, and you will find shoes as well as seasonal clothes. It's good to keep an eye on their socials, as they often have 'everything for 400 HUF' days, which means you can get excellent pieces for roughly one euro.

Vintage Shop Práter

1083, Práter u. 9, Józsefváros, insta @vintageshopprater

Coming into this vintage shop is like entering the dressing room of a theatre: this small, and therefore very crowded shop has an impressive collection of ball gowns, skirts, top hats, coats, blouses, furs, jewellery, and a wedding gown heaven on the second floor. All vintage of course, most of them from Hungary, but with many items from Austria and Germany, too.

Bazáruház

1095, Dandár u. 29,
Ferencváros,
fb @antikbazaruhaz.
regiseg

Bazáruháza is a shop that is like a flea market in itself. It is not that big but completely packed floor to ceiling with lots of hidden treasures waiting to be found. Strange items and antiques from Hungary, but also some post-Soviet andCold War era memorabilia, ceramics, paintings, and so much more. Prices are very reasonable so you probably won't leave this shop empty handed.

↓ SZPUTNYIK

STREETWEAR

Balázs' kicks

*1052, Károly krt. 24,
Belváros, balazskicks.com*

Balázs, the man himself, has become something of a local celebrity with his rare kicks. He stocks the major brands, but only the special editions.

Tisza cipő

*1075, Károly krt. 1,
Belváros, tiszacipo.hu*

In the 1970s, everyone owned a pair of Tisza trainers, but it was only after a major image change in 2003 that the company became a hip, local, high-end streetwear brand.

[UNREAL]

*1052, Petőfi Sándor u. 10,
Belváros,
unrealindustries.com*

[UNREAL] puts a new perspective on high-end streetwear by holding a mirror to daily life. The fashion lines they have released so far each tackled an aspect of classical art or science, such as The Big Bang, The Golden Ratio, and Space and Time.

PSTR Store

*1075, Rumbach
Sebestyén u. 6,
insta @pstrstore*

At PSTR they believe in personal contact and the magic of a brick-and-mortar shop. You can enjoy the atmosphere and major international urban brands such as Dickies, Pieces, and Kangol in two locations close to one another. They also sell a curated selection of vintage items.

Raktaar Music and Clothing Store

1075, Madách Imre út 8, Belváros, raktaar.hu

Raktaar is both a record shop and streetwear store, with the latter featuring a collection of selected designers, such as the Hungarian Hidegvér, and familiar brands Carhartt WIP, and Obey. AKT Records, managing the music section of the shop, focuses on electronic music.

Rdrop Sneaker Store

1051, Hercegprímás u. 12, Belváros, rdrop.hu

Here you will find all the major sneaker brands, as well as apparel by international makers such as Denim Tears, SP5DER, Hellstar, and KAWS. Their in-store service is excellent.

Store 13 Pest

1061, Király u. 52, Belváros, store13.hu

A true skate and snowboard shop, stocking all major brands. Apart from clothes, they sell skateboards and snowboards, as well as other accessories for your favourite sports.

Lollipop Factory

1061, Király u. 24, Belváros, lollipopbudapest.com

Lollipop mainly stocks local designer brands and upcycled urban fashion. The shop is a colourful, happy collection of clothes and accessories, with lively music and eccentric vibes.

Kazetta Café & Showroom

1023, Török u. 3, Óbuda, insta @kazettacafe

A venture by a young couple designing their own streetwear under the name of Kazetta, on display in a cosy café they run as well, serving speciality coffee by local coffee lab Goosebumps.

BUDAPEST FASHION

Nanushka

1052, Bécsi u. 3, Belváros, nanushka.com

Founded by Sandra Sándor, Nanushka focuses on responsible fashion, aiming for minimal environmental impact. They have a range of men's and women's fashion wear and accessories of modern elegance for all occasions.

DAS Fanni Kimono

1054, Szemere u. 9, Belváros, dasfannikimono.com

This traditional Japanese garment is brought back into style by local designer brand DAS Fanni. With a range of fabrics and prints, and different lengths and designs, she makes the perfect forever-piece for everyday wear or for a special occasion. The showroom is open by appointment only.

Kamchatka Design

1056, Nyári Pál u. 7, Belváros, fb @kamchatkadesign

For elegant but comfortable, and most importantly colourful, women's fashion, go to Kamchatka. All made in the workshop at the back of the showroom.

Wonderlab

1053, Veres Pálné u. 3, Belváros, wonderlabconcept.com

A small concept store with a large range of products. Whether it's for yourself, a friend or your dog, you can choose from excellent, high-end Hungarian fashion designer brands.

NUBU

1061, Andrássy út 15, Belváros, nubu.hu

Mostly monochrome design elements, their timeless pieces are both comfortable and functional.

Tomcsanyi

1061, Paulay Ede u. 41, Belváros, tomcsanyi.eu

Budapest-based designer Dóri Tomcsányi creates contemporary womenswear in which she weaves traditional motifs and unexpected elements, such as fireflies or plastic chairs. Her unique, colourful style makes her pieces instantly recognisable. Showroom open by appointment only.

Medencebag

1118, Ménesi u. 1, Újbuda, medencebag.com

If you are looking for a practical, cool and above all sustainable backpack, Medence is the one for you. They use upcycled materials such as billboards and leftover fabric to create one-off bags. You can even make your own bag during one of their workshops.

Printa

1075, Rumbach Sebestyén u. 10, Belváros, printa.hu

Printa sells local fashion and home deco made with a low environmental impact while remaining ultimately stylish. The Hungarian countryside is a recurring motif in their art, and they also have a collection dedicated to Budapest.

Mono Art & Design

1053, Kossuth Lajos u. 12, Belváros, fb @monoartanddesign

This concept store sells high-end fashion and interior art pieces, as well as outsider art, thereby supporting a good cause. You can browse their collection in their large showroom in the city centre.

Tipton Eyeworks

1092, Erkel u. 6, Ferencváros, tiptoneyeworks.com

If you've been wearing glasses your whole life, there's likely little that could surprise you. But at Tipton, they make glasses from vinyl in all shapes and colours. At their showroom, they also have several other brands on display.

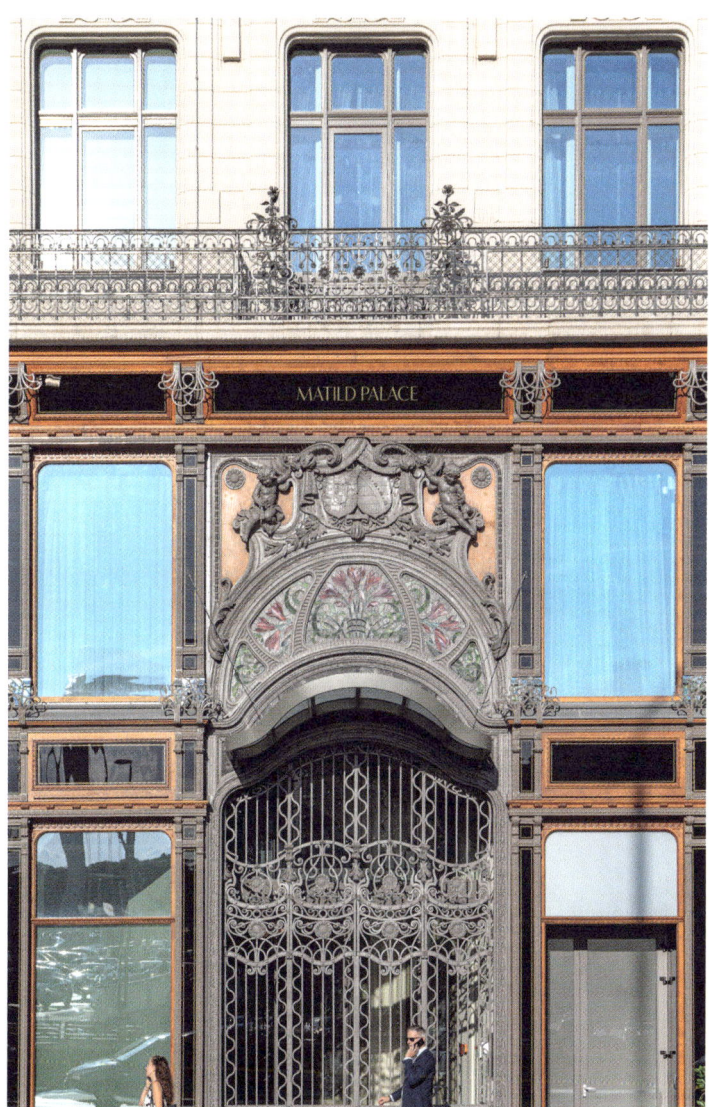

BOOKSHOPS

Massolit

1072, Nagy Diófa u. 30,
Belváros,
fb @massolitbudapest

Massolit is like a tranquil island in the bustling city centre. It is a cosy café and English-language bookshop, with a rich selection of translated Hungarian titles, new editions, and second-hand books, where you can sit and work or read while enjoying your coffee and cake. The garden in the back is a great way of escaping the buzz of the streets and just taking a break in the greenery.

Bestsellers

1051, Október 6. u. 11,
Belváros, bestsellers.hu

Bestsellers has the largest selection of books in different languages. They always stock the latest releases and also sell newspapers and magazines. You can find some games and gift items at the shop too.

Libra

1085, Kölcsey u. 2,
Belváros,
nyelvkonyvbolt.hu

The two Libra shops on either side of the road both sell books on language acquisition, as well as foreign literature. The largest of the two focuses solely on English, while the other has a collection of books in other languages, such as German, Italian, and French. The latter also has a little café.

Atlantis

1061, Király u. 2, Belváros, atlantiszkiado.hu

While only a section of the bookshop is reserved for English-language books, they usually have a great collection of classic literature, modern paperbacks, and art books. They usually also have a small selection of graphic novels.

Fuga

1052, Petőfi Sándor u. 5, Belváros, fuga.org.hu

Apart from being an exhibition centre for architecture-based art, Fuga also has a significant bookshop that sells many English-language photography books and works on architecture. It's the place to be if you are interested in this aspect of Budapest.

Bookshops on Múzeum korut

1053, Múzeum krt. 13-15, 27, 35, Belváros, kozpontiantikvarium.hu, fb @ weoressandorantikvarium, muzeumantikvarium.hu

Opposite the National Museum, the street is packed with small second-hand bookshops. While these mostly focus on a Hungarian audience, most of them will have a few shelves reserved for English-language books. Especially Weöres Sándor Antikvárium, with its piles of books you need to manoeuvre around, is worth a peek. In it, you will find the English-language section on the far end of the little shop. Központi Antikvárium is the largest and likely stocks the widest range of antique books, maps, and a variety of genres. Múzeum Antikvárium has some nice, rare, old volumes in their foreign language section that are interesting to check out, too.

Eiffel Antikvárium

1062, Nyugati Pályaudvar, fb @eiffelantikvarium

In the subway leading to Nyugati Railway Station, there is a hidden little second-hand bookshop. It might look shabby from the outside, but sometimes you can strike gold there. The English-language section is only a couple of shelves, but worth checking out if you are in the neighbourhood.

Di-Plant

1085, Gyulai Pál u. 16, Belváros, diplant-nyelvkonyvbolt.hu

Even though Di-Plant mostly focuses on teaching and learning modules for English as a second language, they have a good selection of literary works too. The owner, usually present in the shop, is a kind gentleman who is more than happy to help and chat.

Second-hand book stalls

all around the city

Scattered around the city, you will come across second-hand book stalls, usually the kind that would have needed a horse to be pulled around town. Stalls like these will always have a foreign-language section, where you can buy books for a couple of hundred forints.

↓ MASSOLIT

↓ BESTSELLERS

↓ MASSOLIT

ART SUPPLIES

BOMO Art

1013, Ybl Miklós tér 2, Buda Castle District

BOMO Art is instantly recognisable for its distinguished style and has become a well-known local brand of beautiful stationery. Their signature products are their leather-bound notebooks and planners. Many shops stock them, but it's always best to go straight to the source.

Fiók Shop

1111, Csiky u. 1, Újbuda, fiok.net

Whether you need fun or professional art supplies, Fiók will help you out. They stock a wide selection of brands, as well as local artists and designers, and even some other gift items, like sunglasses, insulated water bottles, and scented candles — all locally made!

Grafit

1111, Budafoki út 7, Újbuda, officetools.hu

With the Technical University of Budapest as their neighbour and young architecture students roaming around looking for art supplies, Grafit offers professional help and meets your basic stationery needs.

Lúd Labor

1072, Klauzál u. 31, Belváros, ludlabor.com

Lúd Labor (Goose Lab) is the physical shop behind the charming paper art brand Papetri. Mimi, who channels her creativity into her notebooks, planners, stickers, postcards, and much more, can often be found in the shop herself, and if you meet her there, she'll gladly tell you about her work and help you make the best choice. Lúd Labor also stocks additional brands by local designers.

AFFORDABLE ART

Prezent

*1013, Döbrentei u. 16,
Buda Castle District,
prezentbudapest.hu*

As small as Prezent is, it has a lovely collection of both women's and men's fashion, jewellery by Shalleszter, other giftable art and, best of all, it is the only shop that stocks the amazing Blind Chic brand with their unique backpacks.

↓ RODODENDRON ART & DESIGN SHOP

Rododendron art & design shop

1052, Károly krt. 22, Belváros, rodoart.com

Rododendron stocks a broad selection of local designer brands and items – from socks, bags and jewellery to notebooks, prints, and scented candles. Recently, they have opened a small section with pre-loved items that are fun to browse.

Paloma Art Space

1053, Kossuth Lajos u. 14-16, Belváros, palomaartspace.hu

In this old courtyard, sheltered from the busy street, a variety of local designers have set up shop, from leather and knitwear to jewellery and home deco. If the choice is too overwhelming, make sure to at least check Ihász Emese with her unique silver creations, New Accent with their quirky concrete jewellery, reFiore with their timeless and stylish clothes, and the happy bags of GabolinoArt.

Szimpla Design Shop

1075, Kazincy u. 14, Belváros, szimpladesign.com palomaartspace.hu

Next to a popular ruin bar, you will find this small design shop with fun gift ideas, the cutest of which are probably the Yetibocis ('yeti cows'), whimsical, furry creatures that you can only find at Szimpla Design Shop. Their other signature item to check out are the 'light traps' – colourful glass decoration pieces to hang in front of your windows.

VINYL & CDs

MG Records

1092, Üllői út 31,
Ferencváros, mgrecords.hu

MG Records curates carefully selected music, offering a wide spectrum from across the musical rainbow. Each month, they focus on a different genre, promoting artists you might not otherwise encounter. If you need a break from browsing, have a cup of coffee in their café.

Beat on the Brat Vinyl and Bar

1027, Frankel Léo u. 14, Buda Castle District, fb @ beatonthebratvinylbar fb @diskoduckshop

What do you get when you combine a mad music collector with his love for socialising? A record store bar! Compact, but inviting, Beat on the Brat even hosts DJs who play their favourite records while you browse their selection or enjoy a refreshing drink.

Wave Music

1065, Révay köz 1/A, Belváros, wave.hu

Run by the most enthusiastic music lover you'll ever meet, Wave Music is a pillar of record shops in Budapest. They always stock the latest releases from around the world, and not just the big names, but also lesser-known, even obscure artists. This is the place to do all your current Hungarian music shopping too.

Lemezkuckó

1077, Király u. 67, Belváros, lemezkucko.hu

Even though *kuckó* means 'little cottage', this record shop is actually quite large. It stocks second-hand as well as new albums from current and vintage artists, Hungarian and international. You'll find vinyl as well as CDs. And for those who still know how to use them, VHS tapes.

Kalóz Records

1088, Bródy Sándor u. 25, Belváros, recordstore.hu

With mostly second-hand albums, you can take all the time you want browsing the various titles in the cosy little shop of Kalóz Records, while good music plays in the background. If you're lucky, the four-legged 'shop assistant' will be in to help you find the album you're looking for.

SHOPS WE LOVE

Szia+

1111, Budafoki út 17a, Újbuda, insta @sziaplus

Szia+ has trendy and affordable designer and fashion items with lots of bling and glam, but also many unconventional items — have you ever burned a candle in the shape of your prime minister's head? — stickers, home deco, accessories, and more.

Kornél

1113, Kosztolányi Dezső tér 4, fb @kosztolanyi4

A combination of art and good coffee, located next to a park with a quaint little lake. With small-scale exhibitions of local artists, postcards, and artwork for sale, it's a lovely place to look for a gift for someone at home — or for yourself.

Líra – Kodály Zoltán Zeneműbolt

1053, Múzeum krt. 17, Belváros, lira.hu

Líra is a chain of bookshops, of which the one on Múzeum körút is highly recommended for its rich selection of new and second-hand sheet music, and music shop located at the back of the store. For this reason, this franchise goes by the name of Zoltán Kodály Music Store.

Sisko Studio

1085, Somogyi Béla u. 18, Belváros, insta @studio_sisko

Not only is this little gem of a concept store full of ideas for you to return with a cliché-free souvenir, but they also regularly host pop-up events and workshops. Apart from that, the first floor houses a tattoo parlour featuring young, talented artists.

Szellemlovas

1067, Szondi u. 18/a, Andrássy Út & Városliget, szellemlovas.hu

If you're looking for a large selection of board games, you've found the holy grail. Not only is this essentially board game heaven, but the staff are very knowledgeable and more than happy to help. You can even take games with you to try them out.

Giháda

1082, Üllői út 52a, Józsefváros, fb @gihadalift

Probably the most extravagant shop in all of Budapest, Giháda is one large party in the form of a punk-rock-goa vintage clothes shop. Not for the faint-hearted, the shop is run by a first-generation punk (who is actually a big softie when you get to know him).

↓ SZIA+

BATHHOUSES

Hungary is a country rich in thermal waters thanks to its favourable balneological and geothermal conditions, which places it fifth on the list of thermal nations worldwide. Moreover, with roughly eighty springs throughout the city, Budapest is the only capital in the world with thermal baths, and therefore bathing culture runs almost as deep among citizens as the waters themselves. The Romans started the tradition, the Ottomans built most of the infrastructure, and the Budapesters are making the most of it, believing in the healing powers of the hot water, which, with its minerals, is believed to be beneficial for muscle and joint pains.

Rudas Bath

1013, Döbrentei tér 9, Buda Castle District, rudasfurdo.hu

One of the best-preserved Turkish baths, which still maintains a strict Men's/Women's Day schedule. The panorama bath that looks out over the Danube is an exceptional experience, particularly enchanting after sundown.

Gellért Bath

1118, Kelenhegyi út 4, Újbuda, gellertfurdo.hu

The breathtaking interior of Gellért is of immeasurable architectural significance, with its pillared arches and detailed mosaics. The concept of a spa day is epitomised here.

↓ SZÉCHENYI BATH

Széchenyi Bath

1146, Állatkerti krt. 9-11, Andrássy út & Városliget, szechenyifurdo.hu

This is the bathhouse you usually see on brochures for the city, and rightfully so. The outdoor bath, in particular, has a lively scene, with elderly citizens playing chess during the day, and the legendary 'sparties' at night.

Dandár Bath

1095, Dandár u. 7, Ferencváros, en.dandarfurdo.hu

Less well-known, which makes you almost certainly the only non-local. A very practical bathhouse that is not trying to be more than what it's supposed to be, but where you can relax, nonetheless.

Lukács Bath

1023, Frankel Leó út 25-29, Buda Hills, lukacsfurdo.hu

Another one of the lesser-known bathhouses, but it has a stately presence. It has links to the nearby hospital, and post-surgery patients come to rehabilitate. The park with its tall sycamores creates a special ambience.

Kifolyó project

1118, Újbuda, valyo.hu/kifolyo

As a result of a grassroots project, an open-air basin was created at the Danube bank on the Buda side, collecting effluent water from Gellért Bath – this way, residents can bathe in the same healing water as the bathhouse's customers, for free.

PARKS

Károlyi kert

1053, Belváros

A true urban park, where young and old enjoy the little green spot in the sea of concrete. There's an inspiring playground, as well as a green field where children can kick a ball, and others can sit and read – and we're sure many couples have started off on one of Károlyi kert's benches.

BATHHOUSES / PARKS

Városliget

1146, Andrássy út & Városliget

The City Park is the second-largest park in Budapest, after Margaret Island, and it has many attractive features that make it a great place to spend time. There is the boating lake in summer, which turns into an ice-skating rink in winter, the Vajdahunyad Castle, various museums, a large playground with a hot-air balloon, a traffic park where children can learn traffic rules hands-on, a running track, and of course lots and lots of green.

Margaret Island

1007, Margaret Island

At almost one square kilometre, with a circumference (and running track) of 5,000 metres, Margaret Island is the largest green area within the city centre. It is therefore a popular spot to go running, dog walking, playing with children, doing yoga, or having a picnic. On the island, there is a small petting zoo with a shelter for birds of prey, a rose garden and a Japanese garden, many playgrounds, and an outdoor water park: Palatinus.

Normafa

1121, Buda Hills

Just one bus ride from the busy city, you'll find yourself at the edge of a forest. Part of the Buda Hills, Normafa was made into a leisure park, surrounded by woods with hiking trails for all to explore. But staying on paved roads is also an option, and accompanied by a hot or cold drink you can walk all the way up to the Elisabeth lookout, the highest point of the city with stunning views. In winter, locals like to come here to go skiing or sledging.

↓ BUDA CASTLE

VEGETARIAN AND VEGAN BUDAPEST

RESTAURANTS AND BISTROS

Vegan Love

1114, Bartók Béla út 9, Újbuda, veganlove.hu

The best vegan street food can be found at Vegan Love. They have all the usual party and fast-food options that you might ever crave, but plant-based. Hamburgers, gyros, hot dogs, loaded fries, and nachos: here you can indulge!

Napfényes Étterem

1053, Ferenciek tere 2, Belváros, napfenyesetterem.hu

If you want to have a proper dinner, Napfényes is an excellent option. They have an elaborate menu with options that a grandmother would probably make for Sunday lunch, but in vegan form. There is also a wide range of plant-based cakes and desserts to choose from. The only downside: caffeine is not on the menu either.

Vegan Garden

1061, Király u. 8-10, Belváros, vegangardenbudapest.com

Hidden in an archway next to busy Király Street, you will find a wide range international cuisine, from pizzas, pastas, and risottos to soups and salads, but also moussaka and a vegan version of the Hungarian *paprikash* are on the menu.

Tökmag

1136, Hollán Ernő u. 5,
fb @tokmagvegan/menu

Tökmag's fully vegan menu has savoury and sweet breakfast dishes, as well as a broad choice of lunch and dinner options, including soups, hamburgers, and lunch boxes. The vegan *strapacska* (dumplings) is a must.

Nemsüti

1054, Hold u. 9, Belváros, nemsuti.hu

Nemsüti offers vegetarian, vegan, and gluten-free lunch menus on weekdays, with daily-changing soups and mains. They have another branch near Jászai Mari tér, but that one can get very crowded.

Szabad

szabadbisztro.hu

Available at two locations, the one in Király utca is definitely the most atmospheric. The food is excellent in both venues, with a daily lunch menu on weekdays, and a bar-food-based menu next to it. Here, you can try some plant-based versions of traditional Hungarian dishes, or just go for one of their hamburgers, where even the patty is homemade.

Kozmosz

1067, Hunyadi tér 11, Andrássy út &
Városliget, vegankozmosz.hu

With a small but steady menu, Kozmosz continues to cater to all vegans who descend into their intimate restaurant. A combination of bar food and traditional Hungarian dishes, it's a good and affordable option to eat dinner or have lunch, maybe even combined with a shot of *pálinka*.

Naspolya Nassolda

1061, Káldy Gyula u. 7, Belváros, naspolya.hu

Apart from excellent vegan and gluten-free cakes, Naspolya Nassolda has delicious ice cream in the summer months. When it comes to cake, their hibiscus, pomegranate, and salty chocolate pie is to die for.

Zabrakadabra

1066, Teréz krt. 28, Belváros, zabrakadabra.com

Zabrakadabra specialises in free-from cakes, so that no-one has to go without. They try to imitate traditional Hungarian cakes in an alternative way, and they succeed: their *Eszterházy* cake is almost indistinguishable from the traditional version.

Napfényes Cukrászat

1065, Bajcsy-Zsilinszky út 65, Belváros, napfenyescukraszat.hu

The confectionery and café of the restaurant by the same name serves vegan and gluten-free cakes and other light bites to take away or enjoy on-site.

Sovány Vigasz Buda

1122, Városmajor u. 28a, Buda Hills, sovanyvigasz.hu

Of all the confectioneries that cater to special diets, Sovány Vigasz stands out. With their amazing cake creations, you really can't tell that what you're having is sugar-, gluten- or even lactose-free. Offering consolation when you are on a special diet, which is exactly what their name means.

NON-FOOD

Pauza

1052, Vitkovics Mihály u. 7, Belváros, pauza.hu

Pauza's motto is: Timeless items for everyday use. It is a wonderful gathering of household utensils of the sustainable kind – anything you might need for your kitchen, bathroom, bedroom, or garden, is likely to be found here.

↓ SZABAD

Ne pazarolj – zero waste shop and café

1027, Fő u. 79, Buda Castle District, nepazarolj.hu

'Don't be wasteful' is the message behind Ne pazarolj's name. Here you can buy almost everything you need packaging-free, such as seeds, flour, muesli, liquid soap, oil, or vinegar.

BIBO – eco lifestyle and coffee shop

1075, Rumbach Sebestyén u. 7, Belváros, bibo.hu

The focus at BIBO lies on ecological products and biodegradable alternatives to everyday items. These include napkins, sponges, and bin bags, as well as personal hygiene products, cleaning liquids, and party supplies.

OUTSIDE OF BUDAPEST

For train timetables and tickets to depart from any of Budapest's four main railway stations, visit *jegy.mav.hu*. For suburban railway services, you can check the Budapest transport website at *bkk.hu*.

Szentendre

Suburban railway line H5 will take you to the artistic town of Szentendre in forty minutes. Situated along the Danube, this outing will allow you to stroll along the river, visit galleries of local artists, and enjoy the best *lángos* of the country.

Nagymaros

As you head north along the Danube, it bends to the West, where it forms the border between Hungary and Slovakia. This Danube bend houses a few quaint villages, with Nagymaros one of them. It is the perfect starting point for hiking in the woods of the Börzsöny Hills, as well as a hub for the artistic and alternative scene. At the heart of it is the lively Piknik Manufaktúra. There, you can enjoy concerts, exhibitions, and great food, all while taking in the view of Visegrád on the other side.

Visegrád

Take the ferry from Nagymaros

The castle of Visegrád stands on top of a hill, looking out over the Danube bend. It was the seat of Hungarian kings in the Middle Ages, and in 1991 the political alliance between Hungary, Slovakia, Czechia, and Poland, known as the Visegrad Group, was formed within its walls. Don't skip the ferry ride from Nagymaros to get to the town.

↓ GÖDÖLLŐ

Cycle around Lake Velence

While most people know of Lake Balaton as an excellent holiday destination, its smaller brother, Lake Velence should not be underestimated. Its proximity to Budapest (only forty minutes by train to Gárdony) means it makes for a great day trip. The villages around the lake, such as Gárdony, Velence, and Pákozd, are great destinations, but we recommend cycling around its 33-kilometer circumference. At a leisurely pace, that can easily be done in three to four hours, which allows you to stop for a plunge in the water. Go to *tekerbringa.hu* for information on local bike rentals.

Sissi Palace of Gödöllő

kiralyikastely.hu/royal-palace-of-godollo.html

Suburban railway line H9 will take you in 45 minutes to the Royal Palace of Gödöllő, Hungary's own Versailles and home to the legacy of Empress Sissi. Here, you can travel back in time and roam the palace gardens and halls like Sissi once did, with guided tours in various languages. You can even dress up like the beloved princess and have your photograph taken in style.

Esztergom

Before King Béla IV moved the royal seat to Buda in the 13th century, Esztergom was Hungary's capital. It's the seat of the Primate of the Catholic Church in Hungary, and only an hour's train ride away. The Danube separates it from Slovakia, which is accessible by a pedestrian bridge. The majestic basilica is a real eye-catcher, and definitely worth a visit. The archbishop of Esztergom used to have the sole right to crown the kings of Hungary.

Eger

Eger is a smaller city about 1.5 hours from Budapest by train, with a very charming and lively city centre and a lot of history. The city's castle, standing on a hilltop, has been bravely and successfully defended against the Ottomans, which still lends notoriety to the city nowadays. You can read all about it in Géza Gárdonyi's historic novel *Eclipse of the Crescent Moon*. The other hills surrounding Eger are famed for their wine production. In the Szépasszonyvölgy (beautiful woman's valley) you can visit various reputable wine cellars.

INDEX

Districts 8
Travel 14
Where to stay 18
Good to know 22
When to travel 28
History 40
Sightseeing 48
Museums 54
Street art 62
Cinema 66
Festivals 70
Things to do 74
Famous people 80
Films & series in and about Budapest 84
Books in & about Budapest 88
Fun facts 94
Photo spots 98
Food and drinks 104
Shopping 140
Green Budapest 172
Outside of Budapest 184

BATHHOUSES 174
Dandár Bath 176
Gellért Bath 174
Kifolyó project 176
Lukács Bath 176
Rudas Bath 174
Széchenyi Bath 176

FOOD AND DRINKS 104
Bakeries 106
Arán Bakery 106
Butter Brothers 107
Három Tarka Macska 106
Manfréd 107
Pékműhely 106
Tibidabo 106
Breakfast & lunch 108
Anyám szerins 109
Cirkusz 109
Franziska 108
Grumpy 108
Szimply 108
Tompa 17 109
Zoska 108
Bring the parents 125
Centrál Grand Café 125
KIOSK 125
Twentysix 125
Cukrászda (cakes & coffee houses) 117
Asztalka 117
Auguszt 117
Dynamo Bake 119
Hisztéria 119
Nándori Cukrászda 119
Ruszwrum 117
Szamos 119
Dinner 120
Arquitecto Pitpti 121
Dobrumba / Marumba / Pingrumba 120
Grinzingi 121
Karcsi Vendéglő 122
Köleves 121
Mazel Tov 121
ODA Bistro 120
Pozsonyi Kisvendéglő 122
Szilvakék Paradicsom 122
Szlovak étterem 122
Lunch 109
Csiga 112
Dagoba 112
Fecske Presszó 111
Hokedli 112
Jedermann 114
Kelet 110
Lumen 111
Műhely Egyetem Café 111
Tosti 112
Zërgë & Wombät 110
Street food & snacks 114
Central market hall 115

Karaván Street Food Court 114
Lángos Papi 114
Molnár kürtöskalács 115
PASTA. 115
Pizzica 115

GOING OUT 126
Clubs 134
A38 137
Akvárium klub 137
AlterEgo 135
Budapest Music Club 138
Doboz 135
Dürer kert 137
Ellátó 135
Fonó Budai Zeneház 137
Gödör 138
Instant-Fogas 134
Morrison's 2 135
Music venues 137
Stifler Ház 135
Turbina 138
Craft beer 130
Élesztő 131
Legfelsöbb Beeróság 132
Mad House 130
Mélypont 131
Monyó Tap House 130
Rizmajer 131
Drinks 132
Bálna 133
Csendes 134
EscoBar 133
Esetleg 133
Hintaló 134
Kiadó kocsma 132
Kis Fecske 133
Kislumen 133
Kisüzem 133
Könyvtár Klub 133
Macska 134
Mikszáth tér 133
Mitzi 132
Rombusz 133
Szatyor bár 132

Tikos a Tilos 133
Warmup Cocktail Bar 134
Ruin pubs & beer 128
Auróra 129
Füge udvar 129
Köleves kert 128
Lámpás 130
Pótkulcs 129
Rácskert 129
Szimpla kert 128

MUSEUMS 54
Aquincum 59
Budapest History Museum 54
CAPA Centre 56
Hall of Arts 57
Hospital in the Rock 55
House of Music Hungary 58
House of Terror 56
Light Art Museum 56
Ludwig Museum 58
Memento Park 59
Museum of Ethnography 58
Museum of Fine Arts 57
National Gallery 54
National Museum 55

PHOTO SPOTS 98
Basilica 102
Chain Bridge & Buda Castle 102
City centre panorama 101
City panorama #1 98
City panorama #2 98
City panorama #3 102
Danube boat tour 101
Danube panorama 101
Parliament Building from Batthyány tér 98
Sunrise at Fisherman's Bastion 98

SHOPPING 140
Affordable art 164
Art supplies 162
Bookshops 158
Atlantis 159
Bestsellers 158

Bookshops on Múzeum korut 159
Di-Plant 160
Eiffel Antikvárium 160
Fuga 159
Libra 158
Massolit 158
Second-hand book stalls 160
Budapest fashion 154
Flea markets, vintage & second hand 144
Bazáruház 149
Budapest Royal Vintage 147
Dressing Room 144
Gozsdu weekend market 144
Humana Vintage Astória & Corvin 148
Jajcica 147
Komondors Vintage Shop, Café & Bar 144
Konfekció 148
LoveBug Vintage 148
LoveChild Vintage 148
Ludovika 146
Narancsliget 147
ReClaim Vintage 147
Retrock Designer Vintage Store 146
Szimpla market 144
Szputnyik 146
Vintage Shop Práter 148
How to dress like a local 142
Shops we love 168
Giháda 169
Kornél 168
Lira 168
Sisko Studio 168
Szellemlovas 169
Szia+ 168
Streetwear 152
Balázs kicks 152
Kazetta Café & Showroom 153
Lollipop Factory 153
PSTR Store 152
Raktaar Music & Clothing Store 153
Rdrop Sneaker Store 153
Store 13 Pest 153
Tisza cipö 152
[UNREAL] 152
Vinyl & CDs 166

SIGHTSEEING 48
Buda Castle & Fisherman's Bastion 48
Central Market Hall 52
Chain Bridge 51
Gellért Hill & Statue of Liberty 49
Heroes' Square & City Park 52
Liberty Square (Szabadság tér) 49
Margaret Hall 53
Parliament Building 50
St. Steven's Basilica 49
Várkert Bazár 48
Višehrad 50

VEGETARIAN & VEGAN BUDAPEST 180
BIBO 183
Kozmosz 181
Namsüti 181
Napfényes Cukrászat 182
Napfényes Étterem 180
Naspolya Nassolda 181
Ne pazaroij 183
Pauza 182
Sovány Vigasz Buda 182
Szabad 181
Tókmag 181
Vegan Garden 180
Vegan Love 180
Zabrakadabra 182

WHERE TO STAY
Charm Hotel Budapest 19
Corvin Point 21
Czakó Bed&Breakfast 18
Flow Spaces 21
Hive Party Hostel, The 20
Maverick Urban Lodge 21
Netizen Budapest Centre 19
Onefam Budapest 20
Paulay Downtown Apartments 19
Shantee House 18
Vagabond SOHO 19
Wombat's City Hostel 18

ABOUT THE AUTHOR

Michaela Bos

Michaela is a Budapest-based musician, interpreter, translator, and teacher. While visiting the city, chances are you'll catch her cycling to one of her favourite cafés to enjoy a cup of coffee or heading to a concert, carrying a cello on her back.

WHY SHOULD I GO TO BUDAPEST
the city you definitely need to visit
before you turn 30 (or 130)

Published in 2025 by mo'media
The Netherlands, momedia.nl

Concept
mo'media

Text and address selection
Michaela Bos

Art direction and illustration design
Jelle F. Post

Editing
Ezra van Wilgenburg, Maaike van
Steekelenburg, and special thanks to
Iris Brans

Photography
Adam Vitez, Roy Bisschops and others

All rights reserved. No part of this publication
may be copied, displayed, extracted,
reproduced, utilised, stored in a retrieval
system or transmitted in any form or by any
means, electronic, mechanical or otherwise
including but not limited to photocopying,
recording, or scanning without the prior
written permission of the publisher.

 Copyright © mo'media BV, 2025

Why Should I Go To Budapest
ISBN 978 94 9333 867 8
NUR 510

Disclaimer
The points of interested mentioned in this
travel guide have been selected by the author.
None of them have been paid for inclusion in
this book: the *Why Should I Go To* book series
is entirely ad-free.

Publisher's Note
Every effort has been made to ensure that
the information in this book is accurate at
the time of going to press. The publisher
welcomes any information or suggestions for
correction or improvement. Please send us an
e-mail at info@momedia.nl.

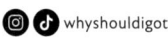 whyshouldigoto

WHY SHOULD I GO TO?
Information on all our travel guides
on **WHYSHOULDIGOTO.COM**

**Why Should I Go To travel guides are available
for the following cities**: Amsterdam, Antwerp,
Barcelona, Berlin, Budapest, Copenhagen, London,
Paris, Prague and Valencia. More cities will be added
soon.